# The Rooms of a Woman's Heart

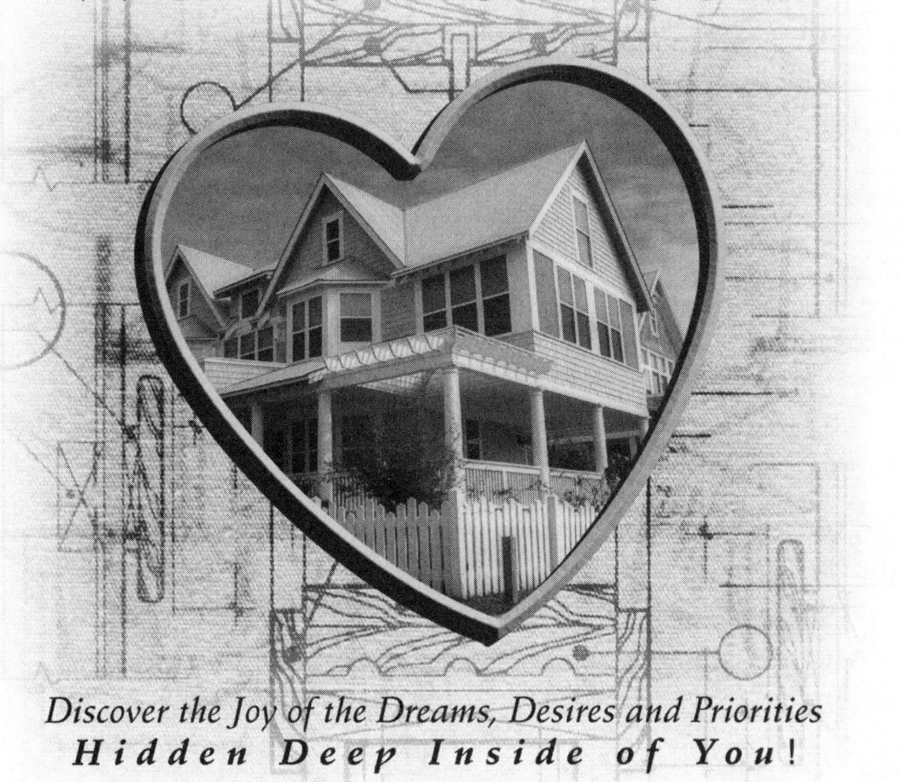

*Discover the Joy of the Dreams, Desires and Priorities*
***Hidden Deep Inside of You!***

Carol McLeod

THE ROOMS OF A WOMAN'S HEART by Carol McLeod
Published by Just Joy Ministries
3210 Southwestern Boulevard
Orchard Park, NY 14127
716-712-0015
*www.justjoyministries.org*



International Standard Book Number: 0-976-48230-4

Printed in the United States of America

***JACKET & INTERIOR DESIGN, BOUND & PRINTED IN USA BY:***
**Eastco Multi Media Solutions, Inc.**
**3646 California Rd.**
**Orchard Park, NY 14127**
***www.eastcomultimedia.com***

**Media consulting and product development by *www.vaughnstreet.com***

# CONTENTS

*Dedication*. . . . . . . . . . . . . . . . . . . . . . . . . iv

*Acknowledgements*. . . . . . . . . . . . . . . . . . . . . . . v

*Introduction:* "Welcome Home!". . . . . . . . . . . . . . . vii

*Chapter 1* A Sure Foundation. . . . . . . . . . . . . . . . 1

*Chapter 2* The Living (or Dying?) Room. . . . . . . . . . 18

*Chapter 3* The Nursery. . . . . . . . . . . . . . . . . . . 41

*Chapter 4* The Weight Room. . . . . . . . . . . . . . . . 77

*Chapter 5* The Kitchen. . . . . . . . . . . . . . . . . . . 93

*Chapter 6* The Dining Room. . . . . . . . . . . . . . . . 117

*Chapter 7* The Family Room. . . . . . . . . . . . . . . . 144

*Chapter 8* The Prayer Closet. . . . . . . . . . . . . . . 166

*Epilogue:* Home – Where Your Story Begins. . . . . . . . 188

# Dedication

***This book is lovingly dedicated to the ones I know the best…and love the most!***

**Craig**
*Love of my life, college sweetheart, and lifetime companion – You stole my heart more than twenty-seven years ago and haven't given it back! I am having the time of my life serving God with you!*

***Matthew Craig***
*My firstborn child - I am so proud of you, not only for what you have accomplished, but most of all for who you are. Your commitment to excellence challenges me...your heart to serve God humbles me.*

***Emily Rose***
*You are the chosen one in our family! You are the girl of our dreams, and I am thrilled that Matt decided to travel through life with you. You are not only my precious new daughter...you are my friend.*

***Christopher***
*I love watching you worship. You bring my worship to higher heights and greater depths. I pray that your life will be one grand symphony of praise! I await with breathless anticipation all that your life will reveal.*

***Jordan Reid***
*You are our miracle. You are the child for whom we prayed and God answered! Although you are in the middle...you are one of a kind! Thank you for being a young man of conviction.*

***Joy-Belle***
*My first daughter – What a gift! The joy of my life is watching you grow into a woman of God. Your sweet spirit and tender ways never cease to inspire me. I'll never know what I did to deserve you...you make my life a song!*

***Joni Rebecca***
*You danced your way into our family with freckles sprinkled across your nose and more giggles than seem to be humanly possible. When I look at you, I am reminded that God loves me enough to surprise me! You have wrapped all of our hearts around your little finger.*

# ACKNOWLEDGMENTS

This book has been my dream since I was old enough to write my name, so there is a lifetime of family and friends to thank...each one so dear and so vital in my life...

The amazing **Burton-Boyce-Townsend** clan – We define the word "family" – at times a bit quirky, but rich in the heritage of godly living and perseverance. See you in Vermont! Save some Ben & Jerry's for me!

**Dawn, Vicki, Irene, and Marilyn** – My North Carolina vanguard: You are always in my heart...always in my thoughts and prayers. Thank you for letting me practice on you.

**Carolyn** – My role model and mentor: I can't imagine life without you.

**Shannon** – My little sister and protégée: Our hearts are knit together.

**Donna** – Thank you for believing in me and for the opportunity to be part of your family.

The **Tuesday Evening Ladies' Bible Study** – BAM! I couldn't love you any more if I tried! You always encourage me to press in to more of Jesus...more of His Word.

**Mary** – Just keep praying for me, OK?

**Sarah, Kelly, Keri, and Andrea** – Younger than me only in years: Thank you for chauffeuring my children, writing songs, Tim Hortons, chocolate chip cookies, and spirits that are like sponges. You make me feel so young!

# ACKNOWLEDGMENTS

The Just Joy! **Board of Directors** – Thank you for your support and prayers. Are you ready for the joy-ride of your life?

**Linda, Melissa, and Julie** – Not a day goes by when I don't thank God for you. Were we crazy that day at Olive Garden or what? Knowing that you are standing behind me takes away all trepidation. Your lives are the dictionary definition of the word "friend".

**Erik Ticen and Matt Gould** – My media gurus, boy geniuses extraordinaire: You have more brownie points with me than you could ever spend!

**Holt Vaughn and the gang at Eastco** – Meeting you was a divine moment in my life. The angels started jumping up and down, and in walked Holt! Let's change the world together!

Most of all – Thank you to my two mothers – **Joan Burton** and **Becky McLeod**: Your lives have been the inspiration for all of these rooms. Thank you for your prayers and your unconditional love. Thank you for the legacy that you have given to me, Mom. Thank you for the legacy that you gave to Craig, Nanny.

In Loving Memory of
Norman Frederic Burton
1921-2002
and
Wesley Malcolm McLeod
1932-2001

# *Introduction*

# WELCOME HOME!

# "WELCOME HOME!"

You might think that your home is 15 Clark Court...or 815 Robin's Lane...or 65 Maple Street. It doesn't matter where you have lived, where you are currently living, or even where you hope to live - none of these historical, real, or imagined addresses are your actual home. Your home has little to do with a street address and has even less to do with a floor plan.

You might think that your home is the childhood house in which you hung stockings, blew out candles, and colored Easter eggs! That home, where you began your journey and where you were shaped, is not your home either. Poets sometimes refer to the homes of our childhood as the place where "life made up its mind." If indeed that is true, then the home of your earliest memories is still not the home of your adult realities.

Your real home - this side of heaven, of course – is your heart. It is the part of you that is really alive, where you live day in and day out. It is where you collect clutter, receive company, fill up trash cans, and then remodel. Your heart is home to your soul and your emotions as well as your thought life. Many people are deceived into believing that their thought life begins in their minds; however, your thought life germinates not in the "gray matter" of your mind but is birthed in your heart. Your attitudes make themselves at home in your heart. What about your habits? Where do they live? Both good and bad habits determine the exact floor plan of your life and can easily be found residing in your heart. Even the dreams that are beyond your wildest imaginations can be found hanging out in your heart.

# "WELCOME HOME!"

Your heart sometimes longs to escape from its earthly address as it feels constrained by the white picket fence that you so lovingly built around the parameters of your life. It is the part of you that is never content with who you are or what you are becoming.

You only share your heart with your dearest friends; after all, you can't trust it with anyone else. Someone who doesn't know you and doesn't love you just may vandalize the place. Some of us, of course, never share our heart with anybody... anytime... anyplace... anywhere.

Your heart is your real home. It is the place where the you that really matters lives life with reckless abandon!

***What's in a Name?***

I have always loved books that have homes with names because somehow, a home with a name seems more important – more prestigious, even more personal. "Tara," in Margaret Mitchell's book, *Gone With the Wind*, was no ordinary domicile. It was a southern plantation filled with the genuine drama of life and romance!

Who can forget "Plumfield" in Louisa May Alcott's classic novel Little Men? "Plumfield" is without a doubt the most fun-filled home in all of literary history! There were children hanging out of every window and door. Life doesn't get any better than a passel full of children in a well-worn home!

My favorite home in all of literature is "Green Gables." Lucy Maud Montgomery painted a masterpiece of a home where the welcome mat was always out and the teakettle was perpetually boiling! Every young girl who has been captivated by the life in Green Gables longs to run through the verdant fields with Anne as she propels herself headfirst into life!

I have a dear friend who lives in a sleek urban high-rise building. Although her longing for marriage and family has been set aside by an extraordinary career in finance, she has not let unfulfilled dreams squelch her creativity in establishing a home Rockwellian in nature. This single friend sends out lacy invitations to English tea parties, decorates with black balloons for significant birthdays, and never hesitates to have her elderly neighbors in for holidays. She has, incidentally, retained her sense of humor as well in naming her lovely apartment, "No Man's Land."

You may not have consciously christened your heart with a name, but the condition of your heart states its identity loud and clear. I have met many women who have decided to name their hearts, "Closed Up and Broken Down." Some women are so prickly that they may as well have put up a "Trespassers Not Allowed!" sign on the front door of their hearts. Maybe the name that fits your heart most appropriately is "Frustrated and Fed Up!"

Whatever the name, your heart is the most precious and eternal part of you. It is the most holy part of you because it is in your heart that Christ lives. For that reason I hope that you have named your heart with thought and conviction, because you should honor His presence with your life each and every day.

# “WELCOME HOME!”

***Cleaning, Remodeling, and Other Dreaded Activities!***

What is living in your heart with Christ? Have you allowed attitudes, habits, and dreams that should not be a part of your life to live side-by-side with Jesus? Maybe your heart needs a good, old-fashioned spring housecleaning due to the clutter that has accumulated or because of the trash that hasn’t been disposed of. Perhaps the worn and out-of-date decorating (that you insist doesn’t look all that bad) shows that your heart has not been tended to!

We may hate housekeeping, but everyone loves it when a home is neat and clean! Truthfully, I’m not a great housekeeper myself. I find no joy in doing dishes, making beds, or cleaning toilets because these are the mundane and necessary tasks of an otherwise spectacular life! I am not a consistent housekeeper, so when company is expected, I am compelled to clean my dusty, messy home until my hands are nearly bleeding! I scrub behind and in toilets, and I become a veritable white tornado! I straighten, mop, and vacuum until the wee hours of the morning so my house sparkles from the kitchen to the bedrooms! I dare you to wear your white gloves into my home - you will not find a miniscule molecule of dust!

I recall once whipping myself into a category 5 cleaning frenzy in anticipation of some long-forgotten company when the Holy Spirit whispered into my heart, “Carol, if you do this for company who comes and visits for only a few hours, what are you presenting to Christ? I think your heart could use a little elbow grease as well!”

# "WELCOME HOME!"

The Holy Spirit gave me a virtual tour of the home in which I had allowed Christ to live. I looked at each room in my heart and saw dust, inappropriate decorations, and personality traits that were not fit for the residence of the King! I was ashamed because I had treated the presence of Christ in my heart with foolish mediocrity and certainly with no importance. As I walked through all of the rooms of my heart with the Holy Spirit as my guide, I critiqued and observed. I applauded very little and must sadly admit that I groaned often and loudly.

***Rooms With a View***

- Jesus pointed out the fact that I had not spent enough time and energy laying the foundation of my life. Laying a sure foundation takes time, pain, and forethought. I saw that I had laid mine in the wrong location and had used faulty materials for the substance of my foundation.

- Jesus tenderly showed me that my living room had instead become my dying room. I saw that I had wallpapered this first room in my home with regrets and memories from long ago.

- I couldn't wait to peek inside the nursery! This is the room set aside for the dreaming of dreams and for the anticipation of all that lies ahead! This room holds the expectation of a future yet unlived!

- The very next room that Jesus took me into was the weight room. This is the room that was much bigger than I anticipated yet perhaps the most profitable room in the entire house. The weight room was filled with the odor of sweat, discarded luggage, and worn-out Bibles.

- I saw that the kitchen is the busiest room in the entire house! If there is clutter or a mess, it is usually found here! The kitchen, though often falling short of the mark, must be a place of priority and of sustenance.

- After seeing the need for the cleaning of the kitchen, I could not wait to feast in the dining room! But it was not nearly what I thought it would be. It was not a place of holiday celebrations or of family gatherings. It boasted no fine china or elegant dinner parties. The dining room appeared as the wilderness of my life!

- After the wilderness experience, I was certainly ready to party and literally danced my way into the family room! I decided that it was time for recreation and entertainment, and I was just the person to plan the party of a lifetime! Have you received your invitation in the mail yet?

- It was time to close the tour of my heart, and Jesus had saved the best for last. We walked up the attic steps together and slowly opened the door of my prayer closet. Though the smallest and least-used room, the prayer closet determines every single element of importance that happens in my heart.

At the end of my very embarrassing tour, I knew that it was time to make some decisions. Did I want to live in this home? Was the price of the home reasonable, or was it too costly? Was I truly willing to maintain the proper upkeep for a profitable investment? I was assured by my Divine Realtor, the Holy Spirit, that Jesus will live in my heart no matter what condition it is in!

However, once Jesus takes residence in my heart and shares my address, He wants to clean until His hands bleed, He wants to paint it the color of pure, white snow, and He longs to redecorate the house that I call home. He will gently move around priorities, set things out for the trash man, and replace every out-dated attitude with His love and joy! Jesus can take a cracked foundation and a dilapidated shack and turn it into a temple! He can take a home that has been literally demolished by the storms of life and rebuild it into a palace fit for the King!

***A Threshold of Joy!***

As you walk through the front door of your heart holding His hand, you will find the place where you belong and that calls your very name. The secret is this: Not only will you be more at home in a sparkling, restored, renewed house...but also, so will Jesus! You see, His goal is to fashion your heart into His home, and as He does, you will find contentment and challenge and be amazed by the wonder and wisdom that He has brought. Most of all, you will find that His presence has filled your home with abiding joy!

# Chapter One

# A SURE FOUNDATION

### *A Sure Foundation*

A young couple, shortly after their marriage, wished to buy a home. While they didn't have a lot of money, they had a lot of energy. They knew that a "fixer-upper" was all that they could afford, and after much research, they found the top realtor in town and went on a hunt for their dream home. Day after day after day, they went out with the world-class realtor and looked at every run-down, vacant house in town. They would look at the windows, the size of the rooms, the cabinetry, and the condition of the bathrooms. Very sure of their priorities, they were intent on not compromising even the smallest desire.

The realtor looked the total picture of success and was dressed in a designer suit with coordinating shoes and hat while brandishing an expensive handbag. After the couple had enthusiastically perused each home, she would quietly take off her gloves, lay her hat and purse on the dilapidated front porch, and crawl under the house. Without fanfare, she would declare, wiping the dirt from her expensive suit, "No, I won't let you buy this house." The young couple stood on the steps of the vacant home while the realtor marched off to her expensive car.

Finally, after weeks of house hunting, the young couple and the realtor came upon a true monstrosity. It was a century-old home that had stood uninhabited for nearly half of those years. The couple stood outside gasping for breath while trying to think of a tactful way to fire the realtor, who, they were convinced, had lost her very successful mind. The realtor quietly climbed under the home, as was her custom. This time, as she crawled out from under the rodent laden home, she said with great joy, "This is it! This is the home for you!"

The Realtor knew a secret that the young couple didn't know. The Realtor knew that it is all about foundation. *Your Foundation Determines What You Have the Capacity to Become.*

> Behold, I intend to build a house for the name of the LORD my God, as the Lord spoke to David my father, saying, "Your son, whom I will set on your throne in your place, he will build the house for My name." – **1 KINGS 5:5**

Your goal in life is to build a house for His name with your very life. It must be a home where He lives and dwells and where glory comes to His name. Every room of this house should reflect Christ's character and should be a tribute to all that He is, all that He has done, and all that He will accomplish in your life.

> Now King Solomon levied forced laborers from all Israel; and the forced laborers numbered 30,000 men. He sent them to Lebanon, 10,000 a month in relays; they were in Lebanon a month and two months at home. And Adoniram was over the forced laborers. Now Solomon had 70,000 transporters, and 80,000 hewers of stone in the mountains, besides Solomon's 3,300 chief deputies who were over the project and who ruled over the people who were doing the work. Then the king commanded, and they quarried great stones, costly stones, to lay the foundation of the house with cut stones. **– 1 KINGS 5:13-17**

From reading this historical account of building the house for the Lord, it becomes quickly clear that building a foundation is hard work! It takes a gargantuan amount of planning and forethought as well as mind-boggling precision, because building a foundation the right way may take thousands and thousands of manhours! Not only does building a sure foundation take more time than you can imagine, but it also requires expensive building supplies.

The foundation of the temple was obviously very important to King Solomon, and it is of utmost importance to your King that the foundation is the strongest component of the structure of your home. Your King doesn't want any second-rate materials in the foundation of your heart, and He certainly does not accept junk on His building sites. Your King requires great stones from which He will fashion costly and cut stones for the work of His foundation.

It is not huge size that matters here. Great or large stones are not what the King requires of you. He only starts with large stones and then begins the process of cutting the stones into a size that He can use. He might not be interested in the best childhood, the most talented, the best marriage, the strongest commitment to church, or even the longest saved! Jesus isn't interested in superlatives - He is interested in value! Man looks at the outward appearance, but God looks at the heart (**See 1 Samuel 16:7.**) That's why the stones only began as large stones, but they were also costly stones.

If you want to lay a solid foundation for your heart, it is going to cost you, and the price will involve some pain. Cutting the great stones down to size is an incredibly painstaking process, but God loves you so much that He is willing to put the effort into you. God doesn't desire to hurt you - He desires to heal you. He doesn't take pleasure in this costly, painful process, but He does take pleasure when He can use you.

God longs to clean our hearts once and for all of our pride

and pretense. Have you ever heard anyone at your church smugly say, "I have the gift of mercy, so I will take care of his need"? Perhaps some saint on the prayer team has made this self-righteous statement, "I am an intercessor, and I have heard from God on the matter!" Mercy is without question a dying commodity even in the church, and intercessors are capable of changing the world! But sometimes even saints of God who have the gift of mercy or who love to pray need to be "cut down to size" by the Lord. Then they will be useful in the foundation of the house of God. It is a dangerous inclination to take pride in a gift that came from God. As things like pride or self-sufficiency begin to creep in, God lovingly looks at His child and tenderly whispers, "It is time to trim off a little of this great stone. It is hard for Me to use you when there is too much of you." It is important to realize that it is not about what we are the best at or what we have the most of; it is not even about our strengths. It is about taking who we are and allowing Him to cut and shape it. It is about the Master Sculptor forming us into who He wants us to be.

Most of us rest securely in the notion that God took care of all of our sins of pride when we were baby Christians. Perhaps you allowed Him to deal with all of your issues in the first few years of your walk with Him. However, if you are anything at all like me, you probably have more issues by now, and although your issues are not His fault, they are His concern. Even Christians who have served Him for decades can benefit from some repolishing or reshaping. Sometimes in a building, a foundation stone may become dislodged, and the whole structure may shift. The same may happen with our lives as we change and our priorities shift, and it is then that the painful work of cutting and foundational work begins again. It is a necessary, continual process to keep our foundations solid and in line.

***God Uses Hard Times So That He Can Use Us***

One thing in my life that I know for sure is that I am called to be a MOM! For the first five years of my journey into motherhood, I was proud that I was a mom and had such a happy life. I had a very happy marriage with two happy little boys. Happy, happy, happy! That was my life!

It was during these years that Craig and I decided that we would like some more children. After five miscarriages and years of infertility, I was struck by the stark realization that I could not do the one thing that a woman was supposed to be able to do: have babies. I could not reproduce, nor could I carry a baby to full term. I could not perform this very natural biological event - unless God intervened! I needed to be refined, and I was being cut to my core. God was reshaping me so that I would fit His purposes.

Cutting always makes a stone more beautiful by revealing its inner character, because the character and color of a stone are never revealed until the stone is cut. God used the inability of my body to reproduce to reveal my inner character. I found that even in the disappointments of life, even in the tragedy of a life not lived, that I could still praise Him! I found that His character never changed in the midst of my pain.

I do not believe miscarriages or infertility are God's will; I believe that God only brings good things into the lives of His children. But I do believe that God uses hard times so that He can use us. God used the tragedy in my life in order to make me more useful. My foundation is so much stronger than it was before the years of infertility. My foundation is also much more beautiful because the cutting of my desires revealed the beauty of His character!

It is the cutting of the stone that causes it to sparkle, because when a stone is cut, it is able to reflect light. When we are cut and shaped by the circumstances and disappointments of life, we eventually will reflect His light. When a Christian goes through a time of cutting (or we may use the analogy of pruning a tree), the response should not be one of panic but rather one of expectation! A Christian should realize that on the other side of cutting are glory, strength, and growth!

There is great importance in even asking the question, "What, in my life, needs cutting in order to reflect His glory?" Allow the Master Builder to shape and reshape and to cut and recut the great stones in your foundation. Allow Him to trim away the excess in your foundation because it will reveal the beauty of your inner character!

### *Strong Foundation, Strong Life*

> In the fourth year the foundation of the house of the LORD was laid, in the month of Ziv. And in the eleventh year, in the month of Bul, which is the eighth month, the house was finished throughout all its parts and according to all its plans. So he was seven years in building it. – **1 KINGS 6:37-38**

It took four years to finish the foundation, yet the building of the House of the Lord took an additional seven years to complete. One thing that I know for sure is that God is not into the prefabricated home business, nor is He a builder of modular homes! God desires quality, and quality takes time! The foundation of this house of glory took over half as much time as the rest of the temple required! Do not be surprised if you have been a Christian for a long time and God is still working on your foundation, because your foundation is important to Him. Your life will only be as strong as your foundation. Remember, what you have the capacity to become all depends on your foundation.

It was not only in the Old Testament that God was concerned about foundations. The New Testament as well emphasizes that one's foundation predicates one's potential. Jesus had reached the peak of the greatest sermon ever preached. It was a Mount Everest moment in the lives of the people listening. They had ascended to the top and were listening to the Great Expositor. Perhaps before Jesus spoke these last few words to the people gathered where the air was thin but the view was breathtaking, Jesus paused. Suppose that Jesus let the silence settle on their hearts after all that He had taught in one grand moment of teaching. Maybe Jesus allowed the hungry people to take in the view, or perhaps He wanted them to pause and not only enjoy the view that they saw with their eyes but also the panoramic scene that He was opening in their hearts. As the followers eagerly anticipated the pregnant words of the One whom they lovingly called "Teacher," Jesus brought the greatest sermon of all time to a stirring conclusion.

> And why do you call Me, "Lord, Lord," and do not do what I say? Everyone who comes to Me and hears My words and acts on them, I will show you whom he is like: he is like a man building a house, who dug deep and laid a foundation on the rock; and when a flood occurred, the torrent burst against that house and could not shake it, because it had been well built. But the one who has heard and has not acted accordingly, is like a man who built a house on the ground without any foundation; and the torrent burst against it and immediately it collapsed, and the ruin of that house was great.
> **– LUKE 6:46-49**

Jesus was an expert both in wisdom and in Scriptures. He had been taught the Scriptures since He was a young boy running the dusty streets of Nazareth, and surely He knew well the proverb that taught, "When the whirlwind passes, the wicked is no more, but the righteous has an everlasting foundation" (Prov. 10:25).

Jesus was also an expert in life. A carpenter and the son of a carpenter, He was probably the grandson of a carpenter as well. Jesus had probably built many homes by the time He was thirty years old. When He spoke of foundations, He knew in a practical sense that of which He spoke. He wasn't just spouting intangible word pictures, but He was teaching from His very own life experience. This was not some allegorical lesson or some far-fetched idea as it may be to us of the twenty-first century. Perhaps Jesus had some dealings with a foolish home builder who demanded to build his brand-new dream home on the sand! In Palestine, there was many a gully that was a pleasant, shaded little hollow in summer, but during the winter this ideal location on which to build became a rushing torrent of vicious water. If a builder were short-sighted, he would lay the foundation in the riverbed and think it suitable. In winter, this masterpiece of first-century architecture would disintegrate like sugar in water. This house would be here today...and gone tomorrow.

The wise man, conversely, would search for rock. The long-sighted builder would travel far and wide looking for a strong, stable, never-changing place on which to lay the foundation. It was much more difficult and made the process much longer, because every wise builder knew that building on the rock took more labor and was more expensive than building on the sand, but the house would stand strong, firm, and secure. There was not even a question if this home would withstand the torrential downpours of Palestine because its foundation was on the rock! A well-asked question is this: Where have you laid the foundation of your life? Have you built your foundation in the sand? Does your foundation perhaps lie smack in the middle of the river gully? Building in the river gully is just so much easier, not to mention the fact that it looks good and takes much less work. Perhaps you have built your life on cultural expectations or, like many others, have built your life on recreation and entertainment. The problem with looking good and working less is that when disappointment comes, when the money runs out, and when people let you down - your foundation is washed down the river. If you have done things your own way for your entire adult life, you have built your life on the sand. If you have built the foundation of your life on emotion-based living - you can kiss that foundation good-bye! Your emotions should have nothing to do with your foundation.

> Trust in the LORD forever, for in GOD the LORD, we have an everlasting Rock.– **ISAIAH 26:4.**

The Bible is very clear about the identity of the Rock upon which we are to build our lives. We are to build our life upon the Rock with a capital "R," and that Rock is Christ. He is the Rock of our salvation and the Rock that is higher than we are (Psalm 61:2). Building a life on the Rock is hard work because it always takes self-discipline and an eye for long-term results, not short-term applause. Building a life on the Rock might just mean saying no to cultural expectations or unhealthy relationships. But, I can guarantee that a life built on the Rock grants eternal rewards!

Jesus said, "Anyone who hears my Words and acts on them is like a man who has built his house upon a rock...." If a rock-solid foundation is the goal of your life, listen to the words of Jesus and not the wiles of your culture. If you want a rock-solid foundation, read the Word of God and not just a popular woman's magazine. If you want a life built upon the Rock, go to Bible study and don't waste your time at bingo. If you want a sure foundation, listen to worship music rather than a popular radio station. If you want a life that withstands the storms of life, hide the Word of God in your heart! You can never get too much of the Word!

Jesus said that *listening* to the Word of God is only the first step. He said that you also have to *act* upon the Word of God if a sure foundation is the goal. If you are only listening to the Word of God, you are only halfway there because doing it is the most important part. Listening to the Word might be likened to choosing the right location on which to build the foundation of your life. But acting on the Word of God is taking the ax or the chisel and going after that spot on the Rock! If all you have is knowledge of the Word, you will become a know-it-all. However, if you have knowledge and then act on it, you become a teacher...a scholar...or even a world-changer! Your knowledge of the Word must become action, and then you will find that your theory of the Word of God becomes your practice, which will ensure that your theology will become the way that you do life!

So - as Jesus told the crowd on the mountaintop - you must hear His Word and then act upon it. You must listen and then you must do. (See James 1:22.) Listening to His Word, hiding it in your heart, and then acting upon it can be summed up in one word: OBEDIENCE!

The primary action that you must do in order to assure a firm foundation in your life is to obey Jesus. When the winds of life blow - and they will - you will not be shaken. And when the storms of life invade - and they will - you will still be standing strong! If you are an obedient Christian...if you love the Word of God...if you can't get enough of the Word...if you have committed the Word of God to memory...if you have committed yourself to be a doer of the Word...then and only then...YOU WILL NOT TOTTER!

> Psalm 104:5 says it this way: "He established the earth upon its foundations, so that it will not totter forever and ever!"

When you do things God's way - and not your way - you will never totter.

*Abstaining From Wickedness*

> Nevertheless, the firm foundation of God stands, having this seal, "The Lord knows those who are His," and, "Everyone who names the name of the Lord is to abstain from wickedness."
> **– 2 TIMOTHY 2:19**

This process of building a foundation is guaranteed to last a lifetime. And not only are we to listen to the Word of God and to obey the Word of God, but we are also to abstain from wickedness. This word wickedness in 2 Timothy 2:19 is the same word used to describe mankind before the flood. It was the word used to describe humanity when God was sorry that He had made them. Wickedness is sin because wickedness is doing anything contrary to the expressed will of God. It is doing anything that contradicts the Word of God.

Gossip is an example of sin that will chip away at your foundation, and self-indulgence causes all kind of cracks in your foundation. If there is unforgiveness in your foundation, it will crack it wide open! Bitterness has the same effect on your foundation as an earthquake.

***Building Materials Fit for a Palace!***

> For we are God's fellow workers; you are God's field, God's building. According to the grace of God which was given to me, like a wise master builder, I laid a foundation, and another is building on it. But each man must be careful how he builds on it. For no man can lay a foundation other than the one which is laid, which is Jesus Christ. Now if any man builds on the foundation with gold, silver, precious stones, wood, hay, straw, each man's work will become evident; for the day will show it because it is to be revealed with fire, and the fire itself will test the quality of each man's work.
> **– 1 CORINTHIANS 3:9-13**

Most of us as Christians start our foundation with Jesus and intend to build our house on the Rock. We use the Word and worship as the key ingredients in our foundation. And then, once the foundation is well under way, we commence to add to the foundation. Some of us choose to add gold or silver or precious stones, while others, once again, make the whole process easier and cheaper and only add wood, hay, or straw to the foundation.

We are not cookie-cutter Christians because each of us is unique and one of a kind in God's eyes. The body of Christ is not one of those boring subdivisions in which every house is the same inside and out. God's children can absolutely not be compared to the type of subdivision in which every lot is the same size and shape! I cringe when I drive through a neighborhood in which every yard is landscaped exactly the same and each floor plan is a clone of the one next door. There is no variety on these streets - just the same...the same...the same. (Are you yawning yet?)

We are all unique! Deliciously so! God allows you to add

upon your foundation with some materials of your own choice. Our uniqueness and individuality come to light as we choose the materials that will complete the foundation that has only been started.

I love pure gold people! Pure gold people are true from the inside out without a shred of guile or hypocrisy. Golden people are givers because life is about others, not themselves. There is not a tad of selfishness in a heart made of pure gold. If you desire to add gold to your foundation, be a giver, not a taker! Golden people are not only givers, but they are also filled with pure joy! Golden people are not phony-baloney. They rarely take notice of their circumstances because they know that sincere joy flows from the throne room of God. If you desire to lay gold upon your foundation, you begin by purposing in your heart: "I will be a person of great joy."

Silver people are faithful servants of God. They serve God no matter the cost or the season, day after day, week after week, year after year. There is not an ounce of show-biz or pretense in silver people, but they are true to the very inner core. Silver people are filled with faith and then choose to be faithful. Silver people are the best Sunday school teachers...the best mother-in-laws...the best friends. Silver people are known by a stronger name. They are known simply as servants.

Precious stones use their talents for God and find great joy in using their gifts to minister in the house of the Lord. They find fulfillment in using their talents in the body of Christ. Precious stones are on the worship team, or they might be the intercessors of the church. Precious stones love to dance and draw and participate in the Christmas musical! Precious stones make the foundation so much more attractive!

Wooden people can be serviceable if they are made to feel appreciated. They are not the first to volunteer, but if asked they just might come and help out once or twice a year. They don't attend church every Sunday, but if they are not too tired or if the weather is good, they will make an effort to be in the house of the Lord. Wooden people have a basically good heart. They are not givers, but they probably tithe. Wooden people are not as strong as gold, not as serviceable as silver, and not as productive as precious stones, but they are still there, nonetheless, and are certainly part of the foundation.

If you are adding hay to the foundation of your heart, it will be scratchy and smelly! You will be one of those in the body who couldn't define the word "tact" if you tried. You may be hurting other people's feelings with your words, your actions, and your attitudes. And, most likely, you are easily offended as well. Hay people are very obvious by their negative odor. Hay is actually only good when in a barn and when eaten by certain animals.

If you are adding straw to your foundation, there will not be much difference between your foundation and that of the hay folks except you will be liked even less by those around you. You serve no purpose in the body of Christ except to gossip and criticize. The pastor prays that you will feel "led by the Lord" to attend the church down the street and that pastor is praying that you'll never come back!

If any man's work which he has built on it remains, he will

> receive a reward. If any man's work is burned up, he will suffer loss; but he himself will be saved, yet so as through fire. Do you not know that you are a temple of God and that the Spirit of God dwells in you? If any man destroys the temple of God, God will destroy him, for the temple of God is holy, and that is what you are.
> – **1 CORINTHIANS 3:14-17**

What have you added to your foundation? This is not a hidden work, because it is going to become evident what you have added when you go through the fire. When you go through a hard time in your life, we will see exactly from what material your foundation is made. When the bank account is low, will you panic or will you trust? When someone hurts your feelings, will you bite back or will you bless? When you lose your job, will you whine or will you worship?

Paul reminds us that our body is the temple of God, which means that your heart is God's dwelling place. You are more precious to God than you could ever realize, and you should never treat yourself as if you had no eternal value. Do not treat your life as if you had no purpose or your foundation as though you had no destiny. God uses us as His dwelling place! He needs to live in us in order to accomplish His plan in the world! Don't you get it yet? Your life is all about Him! Your heart is all about Him! Your foundation is all about Him!

### ***The Finishing Touch***

> Now when the builders had laid the foundation of the temple of the LORD, the priests stood in their apparel with trumpets, and the Levites, the sons of Asaph, with cymbals,

> to praise the LORD according to the directions of King David of Israel. They sang, praising and giving thanks to the LORD, saying, "For He is good, for His lovingkindness is upon Israel forever." And all the people shouted with a great shout when they praised the LORD because the foundation of the house of the LORD was laid. – **EZRA 3:10-11**

Every foundation has to have a time of praise! If you have laid your foundation well, it is time to party! Finish your foundation with a time of thanksgiving. Be a worshiper and tell the Lord often that you love Him! Say thank you to your Master Builder loudly as you lift up your hands and surrender all that you are to all that He is. This is the entire reason that our hearts are His home: that we would become His throne room and that our lives would be filled with praise!

# Chapter Two

# THE LIVING (OR DYING?) ROOM

You have laid a solid and sure foundation in your home and have even built upon the foundation with all kinds of durable, yet aesthetic materials. Now it is time to step into the rooms of this house that you call home. It is time to rediscover each room one at a time. It is time to observe the beauty achieved in each room - or the damage done.

I must warn you: This chapter is not an "easy read," nor will it at first seem to warm your heart. It is in this chapter that helpful and needful major reconstruction may have to be done on this room of your heart. The Master Builder is going to tear down some walls, rip up floors, and generally do whatever it takes to replace and renew, refurbish and rebuild. The end result will be a room that sparkles with the awe-inspiring touch and skill that only a true Master Builder and Designer can achieve! At times, the pain may seem enormous, but the results will be incredibly wonderful! Will you read this chapter even though every molecule in your heart might be screaming, "No-o-o-o!"? It's up to you...it may be the choice of your lifetime.

You see, the only to way to abundantly experience the life that God has planned for you is to first face death. As Christians, we face death on a daily - sometimes hourly, and perhaps even by the moment - basis. Every day in my life, self rears its ugly head, and I have to choose living life either my way or God's way. Every hour of my life, I am faced with the dilemma of selfishness of selflessness. Every minute of each hour of every day brings new opportunities to lay down my will, which only brings death to my self-will, in the powerful exchange for His will, which is a sure route to the very life of God!

As you open the front door and begin to walk across the threshold of your home, you might expect to be greeted by a sparkling chandelier or a hallway table adorned with an antique lamp and fresh-cut flowers. Perhaps you anticipated family pictures dearly hung on the walls or shoes of every size and personality lining the entryway. However, this does not describe the very first room in your heart. Surprisingly, the first room in your heart may be known as the dying room where you thought it would be the living room!

Don't panic! This room is not decorated in black, and it does not have a funeral wreath on the door. This dying room is not what it seems...

***The Glitter of the Gutter***

> Lot lifted up his eyes and saw all the valley of the Jordan, that it was well watered everywhere – this was before the Lord destroyed Sodom and Gomorrah – like the garden of the LORD, like the land of Egypt as you go to Zoar. So Lot chose for himself all the valley of the Jordan, and Lot journeyed eastward. Thus they separated from each other.
>
> **– GENESIS 13:10-11**

This is a sad, sad story in the Bible. If you were to read the story of Lot in its entirety, it would be rated R – or may be closer to the dreadful X. It is the story of a man who had chosen the choicest land. He had plenty of herds and cattle, and he had lovely children. But Lot found that life was not what he thought it was, and he had become disappointed with his life choices. This may describe you as well.

At the time, you thought that you were making good choices. You even thought that you were choosing better than good. You were all about choosing the best in life. The grass was oh, so green! You settled your life right in the middle of a picturesque scene of rolling valleys and fertile grasslands. You smugly and eagerly thought, "Surely this is the right spot on which to build my life!"

However, what you did not anticipate was the problem that inevitably follows every time that appearance is chosen over substance. You chose what looked good rather than what God said was good. The painful truth to be learned in this is that the enemy of God's perfect will for your life is often something very, very good. The strategy of our strategic, yet stupid enemy is that rarely will he tempt you with a gutter life. He disguises the gutter with glitter. The devil does not try to sell you a run-down, beaten-up, falling-down shack. He paints the place up a little, and he might even re-carpet the worn-out, stained places. But the fresh paint and new carpet are all part of the lie, and this place is not what it had once seemed to be. As life unraveled itself, it becomes shockingly clear that you had chosen poorly. Then, again, maybe it was not so much that you had chosen poorly but that the situation changed. People had changed. Maybe the grass had truly been green during one season. But now, you are filled with remorse over ghastly choices that seemed right at the time.

### *Change - With a Capital "C"*

> Now the two angels came to Sodom in the evening as Lot was sitting in the gate of Sodom. When Lot saw them, he rose to meet them and bowed down with his face to the ground. And he said, "Now behold, my lords, please turn aside into your servant's house, and spend the night, and wash your feet; then

> you may rise early and go on your way." They said however, "No, but we shall spend the night in the square." Yet he urged them strongly, so they turned aside to him and entered his house; and he prepared a feast for them, and baked unleavened bread, and they ate. – **GENESIS 19:1-3**

Lot was visited by angels! May I remind you that angels are always sent by God? They bring His presence and His message to humanity. Lot had a divine appointment and was taken utterly by surprise! He was honored, and then he showed his delight by his Southern hospitality! He intended to put his best foot forward and impress the socks off these angelic beings!

> When morning dawned, the angels urged Lot, saying, "Up, take your wife and your two daughters who are here, or you will be swept away in the punishment of the city."
> – **GENESIS 19:15**

The angelic beings came not to be impressed by the ritz that was put on by Lot. When the Lord interrupts our lives, He usually does not intend for us to prepare a seven-course meal or pretend to be someone or something that we are not. The reason that the Lord invades our lives is that He comes with a message and for a purpose. A divine appointment usually means Change - with a capital C!

A messenger from God rarely comes to say, "Well done, you good and faithful servant!" An angelic being rarely comes to throw a party in your honor. All of that will happen at the end of your life when your race has been won and your course has been finished. But as long as you are still breathing, God is still talking, challenging, and causing growth in your life.

When God invades our everyday existence with a word, our natural inclination is to prepare a feast and invite Jesus into our dining room. He patiently says, "Not yet, dear one. I have a word for you. Let's leave the dining room and go into the dying room!" God says it is time for a new thing. You might not understand it and might not even agree with the change that He is bringing, but God is calling you to leave the past behind and enter a new season in life. The ability to embrace transition is not a human characteristic. When change comes...and it will...do not assume that you won't require divine strength. Nobody likes transition; most people hate change – especially women. No one likes leaving the past behind.

God loves change because the time of transition inevitably raises us to a new level of trust in Him. When God calls His children out of the rut, out of the ordinary, out of the past, He knows that we will reach the end of our human resources and therefore will cling to the inexhaustible wealth of strength that He has stored up in heaven with our names on it! God likes change, and we must desire what God likes! God loves you enough to do a new thing in your life. The day of the "same ol', same ol'" is forever past. God is calling you to change and to transition. He desires that you leave the past behind.

### *Your Destiny Is Change*

Craig and I lived in rural North Carolina for sixteen years, and I loved my life in the sunny South! I had a beautiful home with an exquisite yard, not to mention incredible friends with kindred spirits. Craig and I both believed that we were raising our children in a healthy, conservative environment. For the first time in our married life, we were not struggling financially. We lived within ten minutes of both of our widowed mothers. This was the place where

I had watched my children from babyhood through the terrific twos and into childhood. Although our two oldest sons were in college, their trophies were still on their dressers and their worn-out sneakers still under their beds! This was their home! Surely God understood that! Our dogs were buried in the backyard, and the basketball hoop had our initials in the cement. We had measured our five children's growth on the doorframe of the kitchen.

And the Lord came to us and said, "Up! Take your family! Go to Buffalo, New York!"

I said, "God, are You crazy or what?!" (Just kidding – I would never say that to God...although I might feel like saying it!) But I did beg and plead with God. I gave God all of the reasons why I was right and He was wrong. (WARNING! Do not do this! Never tell God why YOU are right and HE is wrong. It's not a good idea.) I was arrogant, and I was impudent. I was wrong; God was right.

As my soul was battling with God and my husband was being the epitome of patience, I incredulously asked Craig one evening, "Do you really want to spend the rest of your life in Buffalo?" Craig looked deep within my eyes and lovingly replied, "Honey, I want to spend the rest of my life in God's destiny."

After a statement like that, you can imagine what we did...we moved to Buffalo. We left what I smugly perceived as security. We left my dream home. We left our memories and our mothers. We left the church that we had pioneered together and where our children had given their hearts to Jesus. God was calling, and we were following in spite of the pain. Human anguish never determines the rightness or wrongness of God's divine plan for your life. It is merely a reflection of your inability to embrace transition with His extraordinary strength!

***Your Number Is Up***

All mothers understand the heartache of sending their children off to college. I thought that day would never come. I thought that they would stay little boys forever. But as the years flew by, the boys traded in their teddy bears for ball caps, and exchanged long afternoons of Monopoly games for a chance to drive their dad's car. As graduation day loomed on the horizon, I knew that my number was up. I also knew that I was the mom and that I could manipulate the college of choice. We lived in the Triangle area of Raleigh-Durham and Chapel Hill. Three of the finest colleges in America were within an hour's drive of our home. I could have just whispered the word, and Matt would have found himself at Duke University playing college football. Christopher always loved Carolina Blue, and he would have driven his little green Alero down the 15-501 to the University of North Carolina at Chapel Hill in a New York minute.

I also knew that God had a plan bigger than my heartstrings, so I reluctantly told my sons, "Go to a place of destiny!" I told my young men of God, "Go to a place where you will encounter the voice of God!" I told the boys whom I had discipled for eighteen years, "Go to a place where you will be trained to make a difference for Christ and His kingdom!" I spoke purpose to Matthew and Christopher when I encouraged, "Go to a place where you will find a godly wife!"

Each son drove away. Matthew left on a hot August morning in 1999. He and his dad drove the beloved Jeep Cherokee out of our driveway as I stood in the doorway. Where did eighteen summer vacations go? Where did eighteen birthdays and Christmas mornings go? Two years later, as I stood in the same doorway with new tears streaming down my cheeks, Christopher and his dad drove that Alero out the driveway but never out of my heart. Both boys went to one of the finest Christian universities in America, which just happened to be twelve hundred miles away from our front door.

Was it hard? It was hellacious at best. But – I lived and they flourished! Matthew married the girl of our dreams and graduated summa cum laude with two degrees. They married on our twenty-seventh wedding anniversary, which would have been the fiftieth wedding anniversary of Craig's parents. Christopher is a senior in college, passionate for music and the things of Christ. The girl of his dreams is still around the corner!

***Victims Live in the Past; Victors Live in the Future!***

> But [Lot] hesitated. So the men seized his hand and the hand of his wife and the hands of his two daughters, for the compassion of the LORD was upon him; and they brought him out, and put him outside the city. – **GENESIS 19:16**

We have always trained our children that delayed obedience is disobedience. Lot hesitated. He delayed; therefore, he disobeyed. This is God's word for you: "When God speaks, don't delay!" When God calls you to leave something behind, don't lollygag around. If you stop to pause and review your options, you will only lose ground. Progress stops the moment that you start looking back.

> **Isaiah 43:18** says it like this: "Do not call to mind the former things, or ponder things of the past."

This is a messy issue for many women. We tend to nurse our sorrows and live in a land of "If only's."

"If only I had married someone else..."

"If only I had gone to college..."

"If only my husband had a different job..."

"If only my mom were still alive..."

"If only my children were still little..."

"If only... If only... If only..."

Your dying room will be wallpapered with regrets if you are not careful. There is nothing welcoming about regrets. Your dying room will become a haunted house.

"If only I hadn't been abused as a child..."

"If only my children hadn't rebelled..."

"If only my husband had lived longer..."

It will be obvious if you are a victim or a victor by the way you view your past. You can trust God with your past, so let the past be your history and not your future. It is a lack of trust in God that causes you to live in the past. Many women have so many regrets that the regrets become little landmines in your present and in your future. These miniature landmines are ready to blow at any minute.

The damage that your regrets can do to you and the people around you is inestimable. Your regrets can cripple you forever and render you useless for God's service. We serve a God of compassion, and even though you hesitate - just like Lot – the compassion of the Lord is upon you. God is able to pull you out of your past...out of your regrets...out of your "If only's." He is able to tear that dated wallpaper off your wall!

What if Jesus had hesitated? "Begging Your pardon, Father – Sir, but I am not done discipling the boys yet. Peter has a problem with anger. Judas is immature. John is too emotional. They still need Me!"

What if He had refused the cross? "But, Father, the miracles are so awesome here! Surely You are not done with Me yet!" What if He had bargained with God? "Dad! These are good days! I feel like I am just starting to make a difference! I've got crowds!" Jesus didn't hesitate but trusted His Father with the past and the future. His eyes weren't on His circumstances or His relationships. His heart was set on the Father's purpose for His life.

***Escape for Your Life!***

> When the men had brought them [Lot and his family] outside, one said, "Escape for your life! Do not look behind you, and do not stay anywhere in the valley; escape to the mountains, or you will be swept away." – **GENESIS 19:17**

After the Lord has pulled you out of your disobedience with His compassion, He speaks yet another word to you. This word is not quite so compassionate. This time, the Lord gets in your face and demands, "Escape for your life!" When God calls you to leave the past behind you, it is not because He is mean-spirited or doesn't enjoy your precious memories collection. So many women think that God enjoys sitting on the well-worn couch with them looking at the family scrapbooks, oohing and aahing over days gone by. When God calls you to leave the past behind, it is so that you can live!

Most Christians with heartfelt sincerity desire to leave the devastating issues of life behind. Only emotional martyrs take any joy or consolation in rehearsing foolish mistakes, childhood errors, or immature decisions. It is often the other end of the spectrum of life that causes us to look back. I am haunted by the good things. I am visited by the ghosts of well-fed babies, clean and ready for bed. I have dreams of ballgames won, birthday parties, and family vacations. My heart is pricked with the echoes of laughter and fingerprints on window panes. When my boys went to college, I cried because I wanted them to be ten years old again.

In the summer of 2001, when Christopher's departure for college was only days away, I was overcome with sadness. I sat in my chair one evening, and as I was reading the Bible, I heard his size 13 feet pound down the stairs in his own particular rhythm. I began to cry, knowing that it would not be long before the melody of his presence no longer reverberated in our family's home. On the verge of depression, I cried out to God, "Jesus! I will be OK if you give me a word. I need to hear from You tonight, Lord."

My Bible opened to Isaiah chapter 33. My eyes fell upon verse 6: "And He [the Lord] will be the stability of your times [and seasons of your life]."

This was revelation knowledge from the throne room of God to the dying room of my heart! The Lord is the stability of all of the times and seasons of my life! My children are not my stability! My marriage is not my stability! My home is not my stability! My income is not my stability! And certainly, my memories are not my stability! God was calling me to tap into His superhuman strength where the treasures of life become lost in His presence.

***Valley Dwellers***

As a Christian, I have a choice. I can live in the land of regrets. I can wallpaper my heart with "if only's." I can be paralyzed by past failures and be crippled by the memories of the good old days. Or – I can escape for my life!

If you stay where you are, you will stay in the valley. It is an easy place to be, but it is not the best place to be. God is calling you higher. The angels told Lot, "Escape to the mountains, or you will be swept away!" Your life will have no significance if you don't leave the past behind you. It is time to climb the mountain!

> But Lot said to them, "Oh no, my lords! Now behold, your servant has found favor in your sight, and you have magnified your loving kindness, which you have shown me by saving my life; but I cannot escape to the mountains, for the disaster will overtake me and I will die." – **GENESIS 19:18-19**

Lot was filled with fear at the challenge of climbing the mountain; therefore, his response to God was measured by what he saw in the natural. Lot did not jump at the chance to take the risk of climbing the mountain because he knew that it wouldn't be easy, that he might fall, that he would sweat, that there would be rocks in the way. Lot did not realize that what looked like certain disaster to him looked like life to God!

> Do not call to mind the former things, or ponder things of the past. Behold, I will do something new, now it will spring forth; will you not be aware of it? I will even make a roadway in the wilderness, rivers in the desert. – **ISAIAH 43:18-19**

There is a principle in these verses from Isaiah that is often overlooked by the anticipation of roads in the wilderness and rivers in the desert. In order to experience His miracle-working power in the desert of life, we have been commanded to leave the past behind us. If we want to see His ability to build in the wilderness, we must not even call to mind the former things. You will never see His ability to turn your desert into a fruitful oasis of His presence until you leave behind your regrets, your if-only's, and your longing for the happier days of a different season in your life.

> A voice is calling, "Clear the way for the LORD in the wilderness; make smooth in the desert a highway for our God. Let every valley be lifted up, and every mountain and hill be made low; And let the rough ground become a plain, and the rugged terrain a broad valley. Then the glory of the LORD will be revealed, and all flesh will see it together; for the mouth of the LORD has spoken." – **ISAIAH 40:3-5**

Do you hear God's voice calling your name to clear the way in your wilderness? Do you hear Him encouraging you to smooth out your deserts so that He can work a miracle on your behalf? When you clear the way in your wilderness by pulling out the weeds of the past, the mountains will no longer seem insurmountable! The valleys and the mountains of your life will actually meet in one supernatural event in your life known as the glory of the Lord!

When we lay down our agenda for His omniscience, we will see His glory. When we discover that all things really do work together for good, there will be a taste of glory! When we enter the season in our lives when we no longer call to mind the former things, the glory gives us the strength to become expert mountain climbers!

> Now behold, this town is near enough to flee to, and it is small. Please, let me escape there (is it not small?) that my life may be saved. – **GENESIS 19:20**

Lot is yet entangled in his own desires to talk the heavenly messengers into doing things from a human perspective. Lot wants to live the life that is filled with safety, smallness, and nearness. He finds stability in fleeing to a safe place, a mediocre place. Lot has bought into the mind-set that the place of least risk is the safest place to live out his days. Is that really where you want to live out the rest of your days? Lot was asking for a life of obscurity when God was calling him to the mountain! It is time to reevaluate your requests that you have made to the Lord. Are you asking for obscurity and safety or for miracles on the mountain?

You might think that a small place is going to save you, but a small place will be the place of extinction, not of your salvation. A small place will be your demise. You will be swallowed up in the small places in life.

> He said to him, "Behold, I grant you this request also, not to overthrow the town of which you have spoken. Hurry, escape

> there, for I cannot do anything until you arrive there." Therefore the name of the town was called Zoar [small].
> **– GENESIS 19:21-22**

The angel of the Lord gave Lot his request to save this minute, insignificant town. But what Lot thought was a safe place actually became a place of great pain and regret. Lot received what he thought he wanted, but then he lost everything that he held dear.

> The sun had risen over the earth when Lot came to Zoar. Then the LORD rained on Sodom and Gomorrah brimstone and fire from the LORD out of heaven, and He overthrew those cities, and all the valley, and all the inhabitants of the cities, and what grew on the ground. But his wife, from behind him, looked back, and she became a pillar of salt.
> **– GENESIS 19:23-26**

The view from the small place is the past. When you demand the benefits of your earthly perspective from God, that is exactly what you will receive...the benefits that an earthly perspective will reap in your life. If you want to live in a place where you can either comfort or torment yourself with your past, it will turn you into a useless representation of what God has intended for you. Lot's wife became a pillar of salt and was rendered useless to her family, her friends, and her God. When you focus on the past - both the good and the bad things that life has brought your way - you will be paralyzed as surely as if you were a statue of stone standing as a sentinel in a graveyard.

> Now Abraham rose early in the morning and went to the place where he had stood before the LORD; and he looked down

toward Sodom and Gomorrah, and toward all the land of the valley, and he saw, and behold, the smoke of the land ascended like the smoke of a furnace. Thus it came about, when God destroyed the cities of the valley, that God remembered Abraham, and sent Lot out of the midst of the overthrow, when He overthrew the cities in which Lot lived. Lot went up from Zoar, and stayed in the mountains, and his two daughters with him, for he was afraid to stay in Zoar; and he stayed in a cave, he and his two daughters. – **GENESIS 19:27-30**

Demanding to go to a small place that seems to be a place of safety due to your human perspective will then drive you to a cave-like existence. Your life will become a dark, closed-in domain that has no ability to promote growth. Will you take the advice of the messenger from God (Gen. 19:17) and escape for your life? Will you leave the past behind and allow God to reveal His glory in your life? Lot had a choice, and so do you. Will you learn from Lot's mistakes, or will you be a victim of historical nonchalance? Victims live in the past and victors live in the future!!

### ***The Song of Disappointment***

Matthew, at sixteen months of age, called her "La-La." She was my best friend and the light of all of our lives. She could fix the best fried chicken and mashed potatoes this side of heaven, and she could clean a bathroom with a spit-shine! She would waltz in through the front door, pick up the baby, fold the laundry, and fill our lives, literally, with song. Her given name was "Lynn" - although that quickly faded into a chorus of children, parents, and friends all adopting her as their "La-La." La-La had the voice of an angel (a very powerful angel!) and had translated that song deep down into her heart as well. Lynn had a dream for her life – and that dream was to find the godly man of her dreams, give him her heart, and then have his babies. She wanted babies...lots and lots of babies. As the years rolled by from her twenties to her thirties, Lynn was still single. She did not let that rob her joy, however, and found great purpose and destiny investing herself into a horde of families who used her as Mary Poppins. Lynn loved my babies as if they were her own, and she spoiled them with ice cream cones before dinner, way too many cartoons, and taught them that life was a song to be sung!

My "La-La" rejoiced every time I was pregnant again, handed me crackers during long bouts of nausea, and was in the delivery room with three of my deliveries. I'll never forget the mascara running down her cheeks as she held Jordan, our third son, for the first time. As the tears rolled down her lovely cheeks, she rocked and prayed...and because it was "La-La," she sang to him. "Little boy...little boy...how do you do? Little boy...little boy...I once was like you. I was just that small...wanting all...the world to be true for little girls and little boys like you. And little boy...little boy...how are things this far? Little boy...little boy...I know you'll reach the stars. And little boy...my little boy...that's why I sing this song - 'cause you won't be a little boy for long."

The one thing that Lynn dreamed of...hoped for...begged God for...the desire to have a husband and children of her own remained an elusive oasis in the desert of her life. As she rolled into her forties, it seemed as if the only babies she would ever rock would belong to someone else. Lynn did not give in to the pain or the anguish. She died to her "right" to have her own way and chose God's way of joy and promise! She continued to love other people's children until one day in her early forties, she was surprised as God brought into her life a man of God who treasures every breath that she takes. We all danced at her wedding! It was a wedding filled with friends...with song...with laughter...and with children! The first babies that she had rocked were now young men and young women, but all came to rejoice at the wedding of their "La-La."

Although Lynn was married in her early forties, she yet longed for babies of her own. Several years into her marriage, she and Eldon agreed to pursue adoption. On July 31, 2004, as my first-born son was watching his bride walk down the aisle, Lynn and Eldon were standing in a hotel in South America, watching their precious little MacKenzie Grace being brought down the hallway and into their hearts. As I was giving my son to the girl of his dreams, La-La was embracing, for the very first time, the daughter of her dreams!

Lynn died to her rights, her preferences, and her dreams. And while she was experiencing death after painful death to her self-will, she eventually found herself right in the center of life! Lynn chose to sing and to laugh and to celebrate with her friends – and God chose to bless Lynn because in the midst of death, He is the God of all life!

### *When Dying Becomes Living*

The dying room is the first room of your heart as you enter the front door. As you walk through it, will you leave the past behind? Will you leave behind unrealized dreams and fading memories? Can you say "good riddance" to all of your regrets and if-only's? As you walk through this powerful room, will you take the time to tear the outdated wallpaper off the wall and then keep right on walking? As you leave the dying room and head into the next room, there is a sign over the door that boldly proclaims, "The Best Is Yet to Come!"

This proclamation will ring true in your life if you are bold enough to believe that God is doing a new thing and that He is able to turn the wildernesses of your life into places where His glory is revealed!

As you leave the dying room and reach for the door handle, turn slowly back to see where you have been and what you have just experienced in this room. The miracle of this room is that as you turn to survey the purpose of the dying room, all you will see is goodness and mercy. (See Psalm 23:6.) His goodness and His mercy have been following you the entire journey of your life. Goodness and mercy were with you in the pain and in the pleasure and were shadowing you in the desert and in the wilderness. They were there when the valley met the mountain, and they were your rear guard during the making of the memories and in the good-byes. Goodness and mercy have painted this room a brilliant white that washed away every ounce of regret. There is only one solitary decoration in this room. There are no pictures or mementos of our humanity, because in this room there is the singular stark beauty of a silver cross that hangs without pretense on the whitewashed walls.

There is only entrance to the next room of your heart. You can only get to the following room by going through the dying room. What lies on the other side of the dying room is really the living room! When God breathes new life into your past, it becomes a room filled with breathtaking plants and exotic flowers. This living room is filled with the aroma of a walk in the Garden of Eden with the God who talks to us and calls us by our names. This is a room filled with life!

### *I Wish to See Jesus!*

Jesus has just made His triumphal entry into Jerusalem! The

crowds have praised Him by the waving of palm branches and with shouts of hosanna and blessing. The people who had followed Him during His earthly ministry were filled with anticipation of what would happen next as He entered Jerusalem during the feast of the Passover. Some Greeks had joined the cheering throngs and came to Philip, one of the disciples, and requested to see Jesus. (I just love the words that they spoke to Philip: "Sir, we wish to see Jesus!" What a powerful request! I hope that your life echoes the words of these anonymous Greeks.) When Philip and Andrew came to Jesus and told Him of the request of the Greeks, He responded in a most unusual way. (Have you noticed this quality in Jesus? What you ask may not exactly be what you get!) Jesus said:

> Time's up. The time has come for the Son of Man to be glorified. Listen carefully: Unless a grain of wheat is buried in the ground, dead to the world, it is never any more than a grain of wheat. But if it is buried, it sprouts and reproduces itself many times over. In the same way, anyone who holds on to life just as it is destroys that life. But if you let it go, reckless in your love, you'll have it forever, real and eternal.
> – **JOHN 12:23-25, THE MESSAGE**

These Greeks who came to Jesus, although not part of the inner circle, although not even credentialed by birth or religion, realized the secret to life. They wanted to see Jesus! Are you as wise as these ancient men from Greece? Are you longing to see Jesus, and are you willing to break through cultural and religious barriers in order to catch a glimpse of the One who deserves our worship and the praise of our lives? Do you want to see Jesus in all seasons of your life, or do you want to hang out in the valley and have only a view of your past?

When Jesus was told that there were some people who had

requested an appointment with Him, He responded by saying that if you love your life, you will lose it, but if you want to bear fruit, you first must die. If you want to be a fruit-bearing Christian, first you must die to your desires and passions. If you want to have a front-row seat in the view of your Savior, you must first crucify your preferences and habits as well as ownership over time, money, and relationship issues. But if you are willing to die and to crucify all that you have ever held dear, you will multiply yourself! You will bear fruit for His glory and have a ministry. Your life will outlive itself when you die! But best of all, you will have a view of Jesus that is unobstructed by your view of the past.

This kingdom principle rests on your ability to make the right choice. Do you love your life with the convenience of having it your way and the beauty of the memories and the joy of living in your favorite season, or are you willing to let it go? Are you willing to die in order to make a difference for all of eternity?

Remember that the dying room precedes the living room. Dying always comes before life! The living room is filled with life because it is abundant with the fruit of your choices. The living room is a veritable paradise of promise! There is no ugly, outdated wallpaper in this room, but it is a room made entirely of glass! The sparkling glass gives you a view of life that is rarely given this side of heaven. All you can see in the living room of your heart is promise and presence! Your breathtaking view is of the promise of life and the presence of the Lord!

> "For I know the plans that I have for you," declares the LORD, "plans for welfare and not for calamity to give you a future and a hope." – **JEREMIAH 29:11**

We serve the God of all hope who is the same yesterday, today, and forever. He never changes through all of the seasons of your life. His hope will always take you forward, not backward. Romans 15:13 says, "Now may the God of hope fill you with all joy and peace in believing, so that you will abound in hope by the power of the Holy Spirit."

The will of God for your life is that you would abound in the hope that takes you forward into a life of destiny!

# *Chapter Three*

# THE NURSERY

Sh-h-h-h! Do you hear the lilting strains of “Lullaby and good night...safe with angels’ delight ...”? Do you smell the sweet, soft breath of a baby, so fresh from heaven? Do you feel the quiet peace in this room?

The nursery is my favorite room because everything in this room is new, fresh, and unused. There is nothing complicated about a nursery, and there is no confusion in this room because it is one of the few rooms in the house that exists for one purpose and one purpose alone: to nurture and care for the little one who has just arrived!

Some nurseries are pink and the walls are covered with pictures of future ballerinas. There is lace and ribbon in abundance in this room filled with dolls just waiting to be loved and mothered by a living little doll.

Some nurseries are blue and the walls are covered with pictures of future baseball Hall-of-Famers, teddy bears, ball caps, airplanes, and trains all predicting the life of the little man who will dream his childhood dreams in this room.

Some nurseries are painted the neutral hues of yellow or lavender. When this happens, we just know that the mom and dad couldn’t wait to decorate! They knew that a baby was coming and were so filled with anticipation and excitement that the colors just did not matter. The gender was of no consequence because the preparation took priority!

Who can resist the heart-stopping excitement of a nursery with two or three of each baby item in the room? This room is a veritable carousel of love with two or three cribs, two or three baby swings, and two or three infant seats. These nurseries are characterized by a sweet tiredness and a joy multiplied exponentially. Joy is not multiplied by the number of babies; joy becomes unspeakable with two or three babies. The mama, who is weary beyond words, somehow has the strength to love them all!

The last kind of nursery is the kind that holds no joy or anticipation. This nursery lies empty. Perhaps a baby lived here for a short time and then went on a return trip to heaven. This nursery holds an additional decoration of which the other nurseries were void: a gentle picture of a mother holding a newborn baby. Sadly, the baby has disappeared out of the arms of the one who had memorized every crevice in the little one's sweet form. Or perhaps in this empty nursery, there is no picture of mother and infant. Perhaps the baby never appeared this side of heaven in spite of the parents' great hope and excitement. This nursery lies half-completed...a crib with no sheets and shower gifts left in boxes.

What does the nursery of your heart look like? All of our hearts have a nursery, which is a room set aside for the dreaming of dreams, the anticipation of what our lives will become and the expectation of a future yet unlived. A nursery can just be a hollow shell that becomes a vacuum if it stays empty. No one can decorate the nursery of your heart except you...the one in whom the Holy Spirit has placed a seed of destiny. It is time...probably long past time...to fill the nursery of your heart with hope and expectation. God longs to give you anticipation and faith in abundance. He has placed a seed within you, and it is time to say, "I'm pregnant!"

These are no ordinary, everyday words! How many times in a

woman's life is she able to utter these miraculous, God-induced words? In reality, these two words are sometimes exclaimed with heartfelt joy and anticipation, while at other times, the words are uttered with great regret and embarrassing shame. How long has it been since you have spoken the powerful words, "I'm pregnant!"? I am not actually speaking about pregnancy in the classic sense of the term...you know, the kind where boy meets girl...boy loves girl...boy marries girl...girl says, "I'm pregnant!" and a new life has begun. Do not make the mistake of thinking that all pregnancies are about women with extended abdomens, aching backs, and swollen feet. The kind of pregnancy that comes to full term in the nursery of your heart can be characterized by expectancy, destiny, and hearing God's voice. This was Mary's kind of pregnancy, and it can be your kind of pregnancy as well!

This is the kind of "I'm expecting!" that anticipates more than you have ever dreamed and then being open to possibilities that you could never realize by yourself. The God who chose a virgin girl as the avenue through whom He would miraculously give all of mankind His greatest gift is still impregnating people today. Mary's pregnancy was more than just a little girl on a dusty street in Nazareth who encountered an angel and then gave birth to the Savior of the world! If that was all Mary's pregnancy was about it would have been enough...it would have been more than enough. But we serve a God who is still speaking today and who is still placing His seed of destiny into faulty, apprehensive people just like you and me! You and I are not giving birth to the Messiah, but there is a seed inside of us that was planted by God. When God planted His seed into the womb of Mary...that ordinary, innocent little girl...He was promising the entry of heaven into all of our life's circumstances.

Paul, the great writer of many of the Epistles, presents it this way in Colossians 1:27, ***"Christ in you, the hope of glory."*** When Christ enters your life, your very destiny is changed. He becomes a Seed in your life that will produce eternal results with His hope. It is in the nursery of your heart that you and Christ nurture this hope until the day when you give birth to His purposes in this world. Luke, in his great Gospel narrative, says this, "For nothing will be impossible with God" (Luke 1:37). Without God in your life, some days even breathing seems to be an impossibility; however, when God impregnates you with His power and seed of destiny, the earth is not able to hold all that you and He can accomplish together, and hell can not stop it!

The Bible is filled with stories of pregnancies from Eve to Mary. Each pregnancy in the Bible tells the story of a miracle – because all babies are miracles! There are lessons to be learned from each pregnancy, each conception, each mother, and each baby, because God in His omniscience knew that all women throughout history would listen well to the story of a mother, a baby, and a miracle.

***God Can Use What He Does Not Choose***

Eve is the one woman throughout all of history who is known for a mistake of gargantuan proportions. Songs have been sung about Eve, books have been written, and even plays reenact the tragedy of Eve's life. History has not been kind to Eve, but that is because historians have not taken the time to read "the rest of the story"!

> So the LORD God caused a deep sleep to fall upon the man, and he slept; then He took one of his ribs and closed up the flesh at that place. The LORD God fashioned into a woman the rib which He had taken from the man, and brought her to the

> man. The man said, "This is now bone of my bones, and flesh of my flesh; she shall be called Woman because she was taken out of Man." For this reason a man shall leave his father and his mother, and be joined to his wife; and they shall become one flesh. And the man and his wife were both naked and were not ashamed. – **GENESIS 2:21-25**

These verses recount the story of the earliest surgery in the Bible. God had created animals and birds from dust, but He had created Eve, the woman, from a rib of Adam, the man. Adam was made in the image of God, and Eve shared the identity of Adam. Eve, just as Adam, was gifted with reason and understanding. She was a true partner to him and would be a helpmate throughout all of life. Eve, like Adam, inherited no sin from a previous generation. She was created pure and holy.

Although we were not born into a sinless world like Eve, we were still born with the fingerprint of God on our souls and the breath of heaven in our hearts. When we were conceived in the heart of God, all of life was at our fingertips, and absolutely nothing was out of the realm of possibility. Our lives were in agreement with the words of Luke, knowing that with God nothing shall be impossible! Our lives were like the fresh skin of a newborn child...we had the smell of eternity surrounding our dreams and desires.

Not only was Eve born into a world that was sinless, but also she was born into a perfectly beautiful world with the lush surroundings of nature touched only by the handiwork of God.

The world in which Eve lived was unmarred by sin, war, turmoil, sickness, and rebellion. Eve walked in matchless harmony with God and her husband. Eve never nagged Adam, and Adam always took out the trash! Eve was not plagued by fears, worries, or unmet expectations. The bills were always paid, and she did not have a mother-in-law who cooked better than she did!

> When the woman saw that the tree was good for food, and that it was a delight to the eyes, and that the tree was desirable to make one wise, she took from its fruit and ate; and she gave also to her husband with her, and he ate. – **GENESIS 3:6**

There is no way to imagine from an earthy perspective what was going on in the heavenlies at this moment in history. At this exact second, the Civil War had begun that would pit Satan against humanity, husband against wife, child against parent, and good against evil for all of written history.

"No, Eve! Don't do it! You were made in the image of God!" the angels were probably screaming in one mighty angelic chorus.

"It's OK...just one little bite won't hurt you," the demons snickered gleefully.

"Eve! Remember God's Word! What did God say?" the angels may have declared unashamedly.

"But, Eve, my pretty! It looks so good! You deserve this!" the demons cajoled, knowing how to break down the defenses of a woman.

At this instant in history...as Eve placed the apple in her mouth...as her teeth penetrated the skin of the fruit...as her mouth closed over the flesh of the apple...a door in the heavenlies was opened. Into a previously perfect world...into a garden heretofore filled only with the presence of God...in rushed sin and cancer! Lust and immorality laid claim to the private world located in the heart of every man and every woman. After lust, divorce took its unrightful spot, and on the heels of divorce followed adultery and false vows. Diabetes reared its ugly head and cheered on its cousins arthritis, leukemia, and dementia as they boldly marched in. Anger burst through the gates with pride strutting beside as its companion. Witchcraft and sorcery had been just waiting to enter this world, and in they pranced like two pretentious hyenas on parade. Gluttony entered the world with this historic bite, as did the silent treatment, migraines, gossip, and lack of self-discipline. Eve thought that her one delicious bite would affect only her. How wrong she was! How wrong we are as well when we choose to sin and think that our sin is only about "me." When sin happens, whether in the Garden of Eden or in the garden of your life, the ripple effect knows no limits. Your sin is not about you, but it is about the people in your world that you love the dearest and hurt the most with your lack of judgment.

> Now the man had relations with his wife Eve, and she conceived and gave birth to Cain, and she said, "I have gotten a man child with the help of the LORD." – **GENESIS 4:1**

Eve, the mother of all living - the woman who brought sin into God's perfect world - gave birth to the first dysfunctional family. But even Eve, who bought into the dynamite of sin and its sordid aftereffects, gave God the glory for this child! She said that she had received Cain with the help of the Lord! Eve never lost hope even in her wretched condition. Although she had acted in direct disobedience to the voice of God, still Eve realized that her God was on the throne of her life bringing blessing and destiny!

> Cain told Abel his brother. And it came about when they were in the field, that Cain rose up against Abel his brother and killed him. – **GENESIS 4:8**

Imagine the grief of the mother who loses a child prematurely. Who can imagine the pain of the one who gave birth, with the help of the Lord, only to tragically lose the treasured child? Eve did not have Dr. Dobson to help her through this time of trauma, nor did she have Dr. Phil or a mother who understood her pain. Eve was alone, walking through the devastation of her own choices. Eve knew that she had brought sin into the world and that because of her sin...because of her own lack of judgment...because of her lack of obedience to the God who had lavished her with blessings...that her own son Cain killed her other son, Abel. The blood of Abel may have been on the hands of Cain, but the root cause of the sin pointed back to one person: Eve. Cain killed Abel because of Eve's choice to sin!

> Adam had relations with his wife again; and she gave birth to a son, and named him Seth, for, she said, "God has appointed me another offspring in place of Abel, for Cain killed him."
> – **GENESIS 4:25**

This verse is the final historical mention of Eve in the Bible. In this verse, she gave birth to Seth and, once again, gave glory to God. Eve knew that every breath that she took and every blessing she was given was bestowed from the hand of her God who once had walked with her in the cool of the day in the Garden. Eve remembered His presence and His consummate goodness. God was still on her mind and in her heart though Eve had made tragic choices with horrific consequences. Eve still viewed God as close to her, as loving her, as graciously restoring a son, Seth.

> The son of Enosh, the son of Seth, the son of Adam, the son of God. – **LUKE 3:38**

The redemptive power of God is seen fully in this verse from Luke when it is revealed that Seth is in the ancestry of Jesus! God can always use what He did not choose! Stake your very life upon the verse that boldly proclaims, "And we know that all things work together for good to those who love God, to those who are the called according to His purpose" (Rom. 8:28, NKJV). No matter what mistake you have made in your life...no matter how you have betrayed God and the person that He created you to be...no matter how your sin has impacted other people...God can use you in mighty ways when you give glory to Him! God can give you a new child or a new purpose or a new dream. God can take the fruit of your sin and turn it into the very seed upon which His kingdom is built. The genealogy of Jesus would be incomplete without the birth of Seth. We serve a God who can take plan B and turn it into plan A when we are willing to give Him glory and honor. This is a miracle that humanity cannot comprehend but one that His Divinity takes delight in bestowing!

### *The Wonder of the Wait*

All of Christendom is well-acquainted with the story of Abram and Sarai, who were very old and very childless. The nursery in their tent lay empty and barren, and indeed, Sarai's entire life spoke of barrenness, emptiness, and unfulfilled promises. Sarai's life held such promise at the outset, but somewhere along the way, she had puttered and fizzled out. The palatial home was traded in for a nomadic existence...the great love story became a charade...and the dream of a large, loving family became a phantom dream that laughed in the night.

> And I will make you a great nation, and I will bless you, and make your name great; and so you shall be a blessing.
> – **GENESIS 12:2**

God was speaking blessing and vision to Sarai and Abram in the very midst of their disappointment and pain. When God speaks, He delights in giving hope and purpose when all that is seen with the human eye is barrenness and emptiness. When God spoke these words of a future blessing, Sarai was sixty-five years old and Abram was seventy-five. Imagine their incredulity when God spoke of generations to come! Imagine their outrageous inability to believe God this time due to the absolute ridiculousness of the promise! Sarai and Abram were about to learn that usually when God speaks a dream into the nursery of our hearts, it is humanly impossible to conceive! Sarai and Abram did not have the assurance of knowing the words of Luke, "But with God all things are possible!" From our vantage point in historical order, we know the Scripture, we can quote miracle after miracle from the Bible, and yet still, like Abram and Sarai, we allow our doubts to conceal our faith. The next time that God asks you to do something humanly impossible, call to mind the words of our predecessor Luke and believe with all of your heart that God is well able to accomplish that which He has called you to do!

> After these things the word of the LORD came to Abram in a

> vision, saying, "Do not fear, Abram, I am a shield to you; your reward shall be very great." Abram said, "O Lord GOD, what will You give me, since I am childless, and the heir of my house is Eliezer of Damascus?" And Abram said, "Since You have given no offspring to me, one born in my house is my heir." Then behold, the word of the LORD came to him, saying, "This man will not be your heir; but one who will come forth from your own body, he shall be your heir." And He took him outside and said, "Now look toward the heavens, and count the stars, if you are able to count them." And He said to him, "So shall your descendants be." Then he believed in the LORD; and He reckoned it to him as righteousness. **– GENESIS 15:1-6**

No modern-day Christian could blame Abram for the impatience that is illustrated in these verses. Not only have years flown by, but decades have passed as well, and Abram is not getting any younger. His biological clock is not just ticking, but it is about to run down! When Abram expresses his lack of patience and his extreme frustration with the unfulfilled promise of God, God does not panic, nor does he give in to Abram's lack of trust. Rather, God, patiently and wisely reaffirms His promise. God is not moved by Abram's lack of patience or by his inability to see the situation from a heavenly perspective. Your impatience does not change the timing of God in your life, and when you begin to compare yourself with those around you, God does not relent. God quietly and tenderly reminds you that He is God and His promises remain true.

> Now Sarai, Abram's wife had borne him no children, and she had an Egyptian maid whose name was Hagar. So Sarai said to Abram, "Now behold, the LORD has prevented me from bearing

children. Please go in to my maid; perhaps I will obtain children through her." And Abram listened to the voice of Sarai.
**– GENESIS 16:1-2**

Reading these verses from a twenty-first century vantage point brings no surprises; however, one must read these verses from the perspective of the Patriarchal Age in Bible history. During this period in time, men were everything and women were nothing. Men ruled with dominance and authority while women were commonly viewed as mere possessions whose only purpose in life was procreation. The fact that Abram actually listened to Sarai and took her advice is incredulous considering the mind-set of the day. The fact that Abram listened to as well as acted upon her input also reflects the type of marriage that this decades-old couple must have nurtured. Abram certainly respected his wife and honored her wisdom in making important decisions. During this exchange, Sarai might have been thinking, "Well, the child will still be Abram's offspring. God did not say that it would be mine. He only said that it would belong to Abram."

History teaches us that marriages during this time were predicated by a marriage contract. The purpose of the contract was chiefly to cover what would happen in the unlikely event that the wife was unable to bear children. Marriage contracts stated that if, after two years, no male heir had been produced by the wife, then the wife would provide one of her female servants for her husband. Most of you have probably digested that last sentence as though it were an encyclopedia entry. Read the sentence again from the perspective of a young bride who was not only dealing with infertility and disappointing her husband month after month, but now had to choose a young maid for her husband to enjoy. The genuine torture that this must have been for a girl married only two years is hard to fathom. Now, read the sentence one more time from the perspective that Abram had not required this decision of Sarai. He had been patient for decades! Abram was a righteous man who truly loved his wife and gave to her the respect due the wife of his youth.

> After Abram had lived ten years in the land of Canaan, Abram's wife Sarai took Hagar the Egyptian, her maid, and gave her to her husband Abram as his wife – **GENESIS 16:3**

Abram and Sarai had spent ten years in the land of Canann when the story takes this unexpected, tragic twist. Sarai is seventy-five years old by now and had probably been married since she was about fifteen. Sarai and Abram had waited nearly sixty years for a child when only two years were required! After waiting for sixty long years, Sarai decided to take things into her own hands and "help God out"! These verses do not reveal that Abram required her handmaid or even requested an alternative manner of conception. All that is revealed is that Sarai took her destiny into her own hands.

> Then they said to him, "Where is Sarah your wife?" And he said, "There, in the tent." He said, "I will surely return to you at this time next year; and behold, Sarah your wife will have a son." And Sarah was listening at the tent door, which was behind him. Now Abraham and Sarah were old, advanced in age; Sarah was past childbearing. Sarah laughed to herself, saying, "After I have become old, shall I have pleasure, my lord being old also?" And the Lord said to Abraham, "Why did Sarah laugh, saying, 'Shall I indeed bear a child, when I am so

old?' Is anything too difficult for the LORD? At the appointed time I will return to you, at this time next year, and Sarah will have a son." – **GENESIS 18:9-14**

Sarah was well past the time in her life when she should have been able to bear a child. She was postmenopausal, postovulatory, and should have been a great-great grandmother many times over in the culture of the day. In short, Sarah was a dried-up prune when it came to feminine issues! There was nothing left in her body with which to conceive! The sheer preposterousness of the promise spoken during this visitation by God caused Sarah to burst out in laughter! Sarah was eighty-nine years old, and she greeted this promise with one meaningful word: "Inconceivable!" The question posed in verse 14 in this chapter resounds through the ages, "Is anything too difficult for the Lord?" Each of us will come to a crossroads in our quest for destiny and purpose where we have to personally answer that question and form our theology on the ability of God to accomplish that which He has promised.

Can God heal cancer? You will never know the answer to that question until you have answered the question, "Is anything too difficult for the Lord?" Can God turn your desert into a place of streams and well-watered growth? Once again, you cannot answer the question until you have settled the issue of, "Is anything too difficult for the Lord?" Is God able to provide when you have lost your job? You will wander around in an emotional quagmire of your own making if you have not answered the question, "Is anything too difficult for the Lord?" The list of possible scenarios goes on and on, but the question remains the same, "Is anything too difficult for the Lord?"

Let your heartfelt answer echo back to God, "Lord, I believe that nothing...absolutely nothing...is too difficult for You!" Speak your belief in the power of God in the face of disappointment, of challenge, and of incredulity! Look your circumstances straight in the eye, and remind them of your theology that causes you to know beyond a shadow of any doubt that, "Nothing is too difficult for God!"

> Then the LORD took note of Sarah as He had said, and the LORD did for Sarah as He had promised. So Sarah conceived and bore a son to Abraham in his old age, at the appointed time of which God had spoken to him....Now Abraham was one hundred years old when his son Isaac was born to him. Sarah said, "God has made laughter for me; everyone who hears will laugh with me." – **GENESIS 21:1-2, 5-6**

When God fulfills His promise to you, when He makes the dreams in the nursery of your heart take on tangible shape and form, the joy will be uncontainable! Everyone around you will rejoice with the laughter of God when you give birth to your destiny! As a mother who long dealt with the issues of infertility, I know of the delirious laughter of which Sarah speaks! Allow me to remind you, you will never experience the joy and the laughter until you have settled the issue of God's ability to deal with impossibility. We honor God when we ask of Him the impossible, because it is in the asking that the believing takes place. Ask God for that which He has promised...believe that He is well able to complete that which He has begun...and then laugh! Laugh until the tears roll down your cheeks and the world starts to spin! Laugh until your sides hurt and your feet dance! With God, nothing shall be impossible!

The story of Sarah and Abraham teaches that there are some things that are just worth waiting for! This is how the prophet Habakkuk expressed it:

> Then the LORD answered me and said, "Record the vision and inscribe it on the tablets, that the one who reads it may run. For the vision is yet for the appointed time; it hastens toward the goal and it will not fail. Though it tarries, wait for it, for it will certainly come, and it will not delay." – **HABAKKUK 2:2-3**

The vision or dream that is germinating within your heart may tarry, but you must wait patiently! Do not be like Sarah and take things into your own hands. You are never too old for God to do a great thing in your life, and you are definitely never too old for your dreams to come true. Life has not passed you by no matter how hard your circumstances will try to convince you otherwise. It is your responsibility to keep the door of the nursery in your heart propped open to the possibility that God just may conceive again!

### *History Belongs to Those Who Pray*

> Now there was a certain man from Ramathaim-zophim from the hill country of Ephraim, and his name was Elkanah the son of Jeroham, the son of Elihu, the son of Tohu, the son of Zuph, an Ephraimiate. He had two wives: the name of one was Hannah and the name of the other Peninnah; and Peninnah had children, but Hannah had no children. – **1 SAMUEL 1:1-2**

Hannah, like Sarah, was barren or childless. The difference between the two women is that at least Sarah had a promise from God for a child, yet Hannah did not even have that! Hannah's husband, Elkanah, had taken another wife probably after the expected two years waiting period because Hannah was unable to conceive. Taking a second wife was never God's way of solving the challenge of infertility, but Elkanah had bought into the culture of the day and would now reap the challenges that his compromise would bring.

> [Hannah's] rival, however, would provoke her bitterly to irritate her, because the LORD had closed her womb. It happened year after year, as often as she went up to the house of the LORD, she would provoke her; so she wept and would not eat.
> **– 1 SAMUEL 1:6-7**

Full of jealousy, slippery as a snake, and not content with her own blessed life, Peninnah bitterly provoked Hannah year after year. With a mean streak as wide as the Mississippi River, she torturously mocked and continuously jabbed at her!

Just as Peninnah made it her goal in life to ridicule and mock Hannah's barrenness, you will have Peninnahs in your life, also. If you have a dream or a goal that is tarrying, do not be surprised when someone in your life torments you!

> Then Hannah rose after eating and drinking in Shiloh. Now Eli the priest was sitting on the seat by the doorpost of the temple of the LORD. She, greatly distressed, prayed to the LORD and wept bitterly. – **1 SAMUEL 1:9-10**

Hannah took her disappointment and impatience to the temple so that she could pour out her heart to God! Hannah did not take her frustration out on Peninnah, although most of us believe that she would have been justified in doing so. Hannah, in verse 10, prayed to the Lord. What a lesson we learn from Hannah's disappointment! Hannah had settled the issue that nothing was impossible for God! She took her heartfelt pain to the altar and beseeched the only One who was able to answer her prayer! [Hannah] made a vow and said,

> "O LORD of hosts, if You will indeed look on the affliction of Your maidservant and remember me, and not forget Your maidservant, but will give Your maidservant a son, then I will give him to the LORD all the days of his life, and a razor shall never come on his head." – **1 SAMUEL 1:11**

This is a significant verse in the quest of Hannah to achieve that for which she was created. Hannah is not bargaining with God in this verse, but she is making a vow - and there is a difference! Hannah is promising God that if He would give her a son, she would raise that boy for Him. She was perhaps reminding God that He needed young men who would not give in to their culture. Maybe Hannah was asking for a son who would benefit her people because the religion of the priests and people had been corrupted during this dark hour in history.

> Now it came about, as she continued praying before the LORD, that Eli was watching her mouth. As for Hannah, she was speaking in her heart, only her lips were moving, but her voice was not heard. So Eli thought she was drunk. Then Eli said to her, "How long will you make yourself drunk? Put away your wine from you." – **1 SAMUEL 1:12-14**

Apparently Eli the priest was used to confronting inebriated people in the temple of God! This was a time of moral decline in the history of Israel, God's chosen nation, and the compromise had reached even the temple of the holy God. When Eli saw a woman so obviously distraught by the circumstances of her life, his first thought was not, "Oh! Look at that precious sister! She is praying!" On the contrary, his first thought was, "That vile hussy! She is drunk."

It is a sad but true fact that when we pray, the world does not understand. It can also be a sad commentary that when we choose to respond not with our emotions but with our spirit, sometimes the church does not understand as well! This exchange between Hannah and Eli is a foreshadowing of another moment in church history when praying people were accused of being drunk! Do not ever be surprised when those around you do not understand your reliance upon the Lord of Hosts just as Eli did not understand Hannah. What Hannah believed was that history belongs to those who pray! This moment in history belongs to Hannah!

> But Hannah replied, "No my lord, I am a woman oppressed in spirit; I have drunk neither wine nor strong drink, but I have poured out my soul before the LORD. Do not consider your maidservant as a worthless woman, for I have spoken until now out of my great concern and provocation." Then Eli answered and said, "Go in peace; and may the God of Israel grant your petition that you have asked of Him." She said, "Let your maidservant find favor in your sight." So the woman went her way and ate, and her face was no longer sad."
> **– 1 SAMUEL 1:15-18**

The change that is seen in Hannah in these verses is remarkable! Hannah knew that prayer would cleanse her emotions and get her back on the right course, and that is what prayer will do for you as well. When you are dealing with a disappointing situation or a perverse person, be like Hannah and linger at the altar. A consistent, abiding prayer life will give you healthy emotional parameters. The secret is to stay in prayer not until you see your prayer request come to fruition, but stay in prayer until you are changed! Hannah came with her requests, but her heart was made whole! That is God's plan for you in prayer – you bring your requests to Him, and then He makes you whole because time spent in the presence of God is always miraculous time!

Eli was the priest in the temple who had observed Hannah in deep prayer. Initially, when Eli observed Hanna's emotional distress, he assumed that she was drunk, but after Hannah explained to Eli that she was praying out of profound disappointment, then he encouraged her in the Lord. Eli told Hannah that God would answer her petition and that she should have peace in her heart. Hannah embraced the words of the priest, and the Scriptures recount that her face was no longer sad. Because Hannah went to God with her pain, God sent an encourager to Hannah. God never changes, and when you go to God with your pain, He will send someone to encourage you as well! God will send someone into your life who will confirm your pregnancy!

> Then they arose early in the morning and worshiped before the LORD, and returned again to their house in Ramah. And Elkanah had relations with Hannah his wife, and the LORD remembered her. – **1 SAMUEL 1:19**

Hannah surely told Elkanah all that the priest had said, and they had reason to worship! Your ability to worship through the pain, through the disappointment, and through the waiting is always the key to a healthy delivery! Hannah is no longer distressed, oppressed, or depressed because she took her request to the altar and left it there. She found miraculous joy in her life and in her circumstances! When you worship, you are acknowledging that even your destiny is about His glory in your life, not about your own productivity. When you worship, you are once again reiterating your firmly held theology that "with God nothing shall be impossible!"

> It came about in due time, after Hannah had conceived, that she gave birth to a son; and she named him Samuel, saying, "Because I have asked him of the LORD." – **1 SAMUEL 1:20**

Samuel, the long-awaited child of Hannah and Elkanah, was born into a very dark time in Jewish history. He was born into the day of the judges when there were no moral absolutes or parameters, and "every man did what was right in his own eyes" (Judg. 17:6; 21:25). Samuel, the little boy of Hannah's heart, became Israel's last judge and anointed the first two kings of Israel, David and Saul. Hannah's destiny was not in just longing for a child, but it was also about effecting history! Her pregnancy was not just about satisfying her maternal instinct but raising a child who would be a world changer. It was about placing the love of God so strongly in Samuel's heart that he would bring the righteousness of God to his culture. The seed that has been planted inside of your spiritual womb is not all about you, but it is about bringing the power of Christ to your culture!

> Now when she had weaned him, she took him up with her, with a three-year-old bull and one ephah of flour and a jug of wine, and brought him to the house of the LORD in Shiloh, although the child was young. Then they slaughtered the bull, and

> brought the boy to Eli. She said, "Oh, my lord! As your soul lives, my lord, I am the woman who stood here beside you, praying to the LORD. For this boy I prayed, and the LORD has given me my petition which I asked of Him. So I have also dedicated him to the LORD; as long as he lives he is dedicated to the LORD." And he worshiped the Lord there. Then Hannah prayed and said, "My heart exults in the LORD!"
> **– 1 SAMUEL 1:24-28; 2:1**

These verses are a heart-wrenching account of Hannah's response to the fulfillment of God's plan, because Hannah had promised God that if He would give her a son, she would raise the boy for God and give the child back to God. The amazing revelation that can be read between every line is that Hannah does not seem to be sad! She was willing to give up the most important thing in her life – that little boy with a cowlick in his hair and freckles dancing across his nose! She was willing to take Samuel, so full of life and joy and so secure in his mother's love, and leave him at the temple with Eli the priest. As they left their home together, I can almost hear the little songs they sang together as Samuel wrapped his chubby arms around his mama's neck. As Hannah prepared for this act of surrender that boldly exclaimed, "God is first in my life," she continued to worship. In 1 Samuel 2, Hannah is filled with inexpressible joy at the surrender of Samuel to the Lord! Hannah knew all along that this pregnancy was not about her desires, but that it was about God's plan!

> Now Samuel was ministering before the LORD, as a boy wearing a linen ephod. And his mother would make him a little robe and bring it to him from year to year when she would come up with her husband to offer the yearly sacrifice. Then Eli would

bless Elkanah and his wife and say, "May the LORD give you children from this woman in place of the one she dedicated to the LORD." And they went to their own home. The Lord visited Hannah; and she conceived and gave birth to three sons and two daughters! And the boy Samuel grew before the LORD.
**– 1 SAMUEL 2:18-21**

Hannah was a patient woman who took her requests to the Lord. She was also a worshiper who exulted in the Lord through all of life's circumstances. Because Hannah had her priorities straight and fulfilled her vow to the Lord, Hannah and Elkanah experienced more than a double blessing! God gave them a blessing magnified five times over by giving them five more children! Our God never changes, and when you do life God's way by keeping your emotions under control and choosing to pray rather than react emotionally, God will bless you abundantly! Hannah only asked for one child, and God gave her six children! God is a God of abundance and blessing and favor! If you want to experience His favor in the nursery of your heart, linger at the altar in worship and wonder! You will receive a blessing that you cannot even begin to imagine! Your nursery will be one of the rooms where the joy is exponential and the purpose abundant!

### *Heavenly Results in an Earthly Home*

In the days of Herod, king of Judea, there was a priest named Zacharias, of the division of Abijah; and he had a wife from the daughters of Aaron, and her name was Elizabeth. They were both righteous in the sight of God, walking blamelessly in all the commandments and requirements of the Lord. **– LUKE 1:5-6**

What a beautiful way to be described in the Bible! Elizabeth and Zacharias were righteous in the sight of God, and they walked blamelessly in all the commandments and requirements of the Lord! Have you discovered the secret that God trusts righteous people with great blessings? However you have chosen to live your life in the past, today is a new day, and it is time to choose righteousness and walk blamelessly! There will be a blessing on your life that will astound you as you choose to do life His way and not your own.

James 5:16 says, "The effectual fervent prayer of a righteous man availeth much" (KJV). When you choose to live your life by the standards set forth in the Word of God, you are going to have an unobstructed pipeline going straight into the throne room of God! God listens and answers when righteous people pray, and the results are unbelievable this side of heaven!

Proverbs 10:30 tells us that "the righteous will never be shaken." Although Elizabeth and Zacharias had no children, because they were righteous, they were not shaken. They went to bed every night believing that God would send a child. They awoke every morning doubt-free, knowing that with God, nothing is impossible!

Galatians 3:11 reminds us that "the righteous man shall live by faith." Elizabeth and Zacharias were righteous in all their ways, and they were living by their faith - not by sight. They knew that God hears the prayers of a righteous man, and therefore they were not shaken.

Righteousness...faith...blameless...not shaken...prayer warriors... yet still, an empty nursery.

> But they had no child, because Elizabeth was barren, and they were both advanced in years. – **LUKE 1:7**

The name Elizabeth means "God is my oath." Elizabeth believed God and had set her oath upon living her life for him. Through all seasons of her life she chose to walk by faith, not by sight, and to believe God! She knew that with God nothing shall be impossible! That is what believing God means: that He is who He says He is and that He can do what He says that He will do. Elizabeth had staked her life upon her belief in God, and she continued to walk righteously all those years of believing by faith. Elizabeth was not impatient with God, and she trusted Him in faith all the days of her life. Elizabeth continued to do the right things, to pray fervently, and to keep good heart attitudes. What are you doing while you are waiting? Are you walking righteously while keeping your eyes on God as opposed to your life's circumstances? Elizabeth was not ruled by her life's circumstances but by her desire to please God with her life!

> Now it happened that while [Zacharias] was performing his priestly service before God in the appointed order of his division, according to the custom of the priestly office, he was chosen by lot to enter the temple of the Lord and burn incense. And the whole multitude of the people were in prayer outside at the hour of the incense offering. And an angel of the Lord appeared to him, standing to the right of the altar of incense. Zacharias was troubled when he saw the angel, and fear gripped him. But the angel said to him, "Do not be afraid, Zacharias, for your petition has been heard, and your wife Elizabeth will bear you a son, and you will give him the name John."
>
> **– LUKE 1:8-13**

Zacharias was in the temple because it was his turn to go into the sacred place of God. He was chosen to go in and offer the sacrifice of incense while the people were in prayer in the outer courts. An angel of the Lord came to Zacharias while he was in the temple and announced that the time had come, after years of barrenness and infertility, for Elizabeth to bear a son.

Elizabeth and Zacharias had never given up, and neither should you give up! Don't ever give up! Be the kind of Christian who knocks and keeps right on knocking on the door of your prayer closet. I have a feeling that Elizabeth had made hundreds of baby blankets and booties in preparation for this little boy, because she was a righteous woman – and righteous women never give up! I think that when Elizabeth saw diapers on sale at the local market, she would go in a buy a few just to prove that she walked by faith and not by sight!

What are you praying for? It might seem that you haven't heard from God in over 400 years! Are you praying for an unsaved spouse or a rebellious child? Are you praying for a job or perhaps a breakthrough in finances? Maybe you are petitioning God concerning a health issue. Just as the angel of the Lord said to Zacharias in verse 13, "God has heard your petition!" God always hears when righteous people pray, and He always hears when people filled with faith come boldly to Him.

> After these days Elizabeth his wife became pregnant, and she kept herself in seclusion for five months, saying, "This is the way the Lord has dealt with me in the days when He looked with favor upon me to take away my disgrace among men."
> **– LUKE 1:24-25**

It was not uncommon for New Testament women to go into

seclusion during the last three months of the pregnancy when they began to be "great with child." However, Elizabeth went into seclusion nearly from the onset of her pregnancy for the entire first five months. Elizabeth knew that this pregnancy was not about her maternal desires, but it was about God's plan at this time in history. Elizabeth entered a season of preparation for the plan of God in her life. Surely she was preparing her heart for motherhood as well and all that this lifestyle change would bring to a mother and a father who were advanced in years. This was certainly a time of thanksgiving and great wonder for Elizabeth as she watched her body grow young again with the bloom of pregnancy! As Elizabeth gazed upon the tiny blankets and little gowns that had been stored for decades, she undoubtedly prayed these words, "Lord, prepare me for what You are preparing for me!" As Elizabeth fingered the sweet baby garments with tears coursing down her wrinkled cheeks, certainly her heart was exclaiming to God, "A miracle! I am actually part of a miracle!" With a heart overflowing with gratitude, Elizabeth was wise, and she immediately changed her lifestyle so that she could have time for worship and prayer. Elizabeth was preparing her heart for the day of delivery.

> Now the time had come for Elizabeth to give birth, and she gave birth to a son. Her neighbors and her relatives heard that the Lord had displayed His great mercy toward her; and they were rejoicing with her – **LUKE 1:57-58**

One can only imagine the joy that was in the home of Zacharias and Elizabeth on this day that their only child, a son, was born. So great was the joy that the home quickly filled with neighbors and relatives bringing casserole dishes, wanting to set eyes on the child that had been in the heart of Elizabeth and Zacharias for years. The true miracle of the story of Elizabeth and Zacharias is not the fact that a baby was born, but the true miracle of the story lies in the truth that they believed God! I do not mean to minimize the birth of John, but always remember that God chose Elizabeth and Zacharias to be part of His plan because they were righteous and because they believed. It was because of their oath to believe that God could answer impossible prayers that God was able to send their son!

### *An Accident...or a Surprise?*

There are no accidents with God, but there are surprises! Mary's pregnancy was certainly one for which the nursery was not ready!

> Now in the sixth month the angel Gabriel was sent from God to a city in Galilee called Nazareth, to a virgin engaged to a man whose name was Joseph, of the descendants of David; and the virgin's name was Mary. And coming in, he said to her, "Greetings, favored one! The Lord is with you." But she was very perplexed at this statement, and kept pondering what kind of salutation this was. The angel said to her, "Do not be afraid, Mary; for you have found favor with God. And behold, you will conceive in your womb and bear a son, and you shall name Him Jesus. He will be great and will be called the Son of the Most High; and the Lord God will give Him the throne of His father David; and He will reign over the house of Jacob forever, and His kingdom will have no end." Mary said to the angel, "How can this be, since I am a virgin?" – **LUKE 1:26-34**

Sweet Mary, a daughter of Nazareth, was experiencing the most delightful time of her young life because she was engaged to a godly young man who had won the blessing of her parents. Mary was certainly not prepared for a celestial visitation and was found to be nearly speechless at the salutation of the angel. The angel greeted Mary as "favored one" and told her that she had found "favor" with God. Then Gabriel, sent from the throne room of God, informed Mary that she would conceive although she was a virgin!

Certainly no one could blame Mary if the thought had crossed her mind, "You call this favor? Unmarried and pregnant? Are you an angel with a twisted sense of humor or what?"

Actually, maybe we are the ones with a twisted sense of favor, because what we think is horrible just may turn out to be wonderful! When God visits us and informs us of His plan, what we do not understand may bring unspeakable joy! What messes up our well-laid plans and possibly a delightful time in our lives just may be His divine handiwork!

> "And behold, even your relative Elizabeth has also conceived a son in her old age; and she who was called barren is now in her sixth month. For nothing will be impossible with God."
> – **LUKE 1:36-37**

There it is again...the reminder that God is well able to accomplish things that seem impossible in our humanity! God specializes in all things thought to be impossible. Have you asked Him for something impossible lately? He loves it when we ask of Him something impossible, because we are honoring His ability to be a miracle-working God!

> And Mary said, "Behold, the bondslave of the Lord; may it be done to me according to your word." And the angel departed from her. – **LUKE 1:38**

Mary had a submissive heart and was willing to lay down every plan for her life in order to honor the high call of God. She told the angel that she was the bondslave of the Lord, which was a significant description of the choice that she had made internally. A bondslave was someone who had been offered their freedom but chose to stay in service to their master. Mary chose to serve God even when she did not understand His plan. Mary chose to be submissive even when the plan of God did not coincide with the plan of Mary. Simply put, Mary had a submissive heart.

Do you quote Luke 1:38 when God asks something hard of you? Do you say to your Savior and Lord, "Behold, the bondslave of the Lord; be it unto me according to your Word"? Or do you whine and complain and stamp your feet as you inform the King of kings and the Lord of lords, "But I did not want pink...I wanted blue!"

"Come on, God! I did not want twins! I did not ask for twins, and You gave them anyway! Can't I ever have it my way? Just once?"

How do you respond when God asks you to love a difficult mother-in-law or raise a special-needs child? When God asks you to serve an unyielding boss, do you harden your heart, or do you serve with love and kindness? When you and your husband disagree on an important issue, do you first nag and then give him the silent treatment? Or do you pray and submit to his plans knowing that in truth, you are the bondslave of the Lord?

### *A Seed of Destiny in All of Us*

Five different mothers...five different circumstances...five different children...but one God who never changes! Allow the lessons learned from these five unique women to change your life and the manner in which you perceive your destiny.

Eve taught us that God can use us no matter how sordid the past. God clearly shows us through the life of Eve that He can use what He does not choose.

The life of Sarah taught us to be patient and not to take things into our own hands when God's time table does not match with ours. Through the story of Sarah and Abraham we gained a theology based on a biblical foundation that with God nothing is impossible! Also, Sarah showed us firsthand that you are never too old to be pregnant!

The poignant life of Hannah is a lucid illustration that although others may come against you, history belongs to those who pray! Through the sacrifice of the child Samuel, Hannah showed us that our pregnancy is not about our maternal instincts but about God's plan for the world.

The words describing Elizabeth in the Bible called us to a higher level of righteousness and faith and compelled us to believe God no matter what our circumstances may be. Elizabeth also taught us the lesson concerning the importance of preparing our hearts for what God has prepared for us.

The announcement of Mary's unexpected pregnancy reminds us all that what we think is horrible just may turn out to be wonderful! Mary's tender heart of submission encourages us to be submissive to God's ways and plans even when they do not match up with our plans.

***When Ordinary Becomes Extraordinary!***

Would you like to be pregnant? Is it your desire to be pregnant with the seed of God? The way to become pregnant is to know God in the biblical sense!

Genesis 4:1 recounts the fact that Adam had relations with his wife, Eve. Elkanah had relations with his wife, Hannah, as recounted in 1 Samuel 1:19. You must have a relationship with God, or you will stand no chance of giving birth to a dream or to destiny. You have to be intimate with your God and spend time with Him...alone! If your desire is to be pregnant with a seed planted by God, you must get rid of all distractions and just be with Him! He loves being with you; it is His favorite thing to do. God longs to talk to His children and to impart vision and destiny. Perhaps the reason that you do not have vision is because you do not know God and are not intimate with Him.

Psalm 37:4 says, "Delight yourself in the LORD; and He will give you the desires of your heart." When you spend time in His presence and just delight in all that He is, the Lord will actually place desire, dreams, and destiny in your heart. It is not necessarily that He *fulfills* your desires, but rather that He *places* His desires *in* your heart.

After you are sure of the fact that you know God and that you are delighting in His presence, then you need to make very certain that you are ovulating. Usually, in cases of infertility, the problem with conception can be traced back to the biological fact that the woman is not ovulating. Do you know what it means to ovulate? It means having faith the size of a mustard seed! If you want to be pregnant with the destiny of God in your life, you must have faith and give God something to work with! Jesus told His disciples in Matthew 17:20 that the only faith that is required for a miracle is faith that is about the size of a mustard seed. In the days when Jesus was walking on earth, the mustard seed was the smallest seed known to mankind. Jesus said that if we would have faith only the size of a miniscule seed, then we would be able to move mountains with our faith!

If you want to fill up the nursery of your heart, then stir up your faith and be positive! Learn to live in constant expectation and anticipation! When we worship God in spite of our pain, disappointment, and impatience, we stir up our faith. When we worship, we take our eyes off the impossibility and place our hearts on His ability to perform miraculous events. Our garment of praise actually becomes maternity clothes because a seed of faith has been planted in our barren wombs.

"'There is hope for your future,' declares the LORD" (Jer. 31:17). I love that verse because it serves as a constant reminder to me that the Lord is a God of encouragement and the God of all hope. Hopelessness happens when I embrace my circumstances rather than His presence. If you want to be pregnant with God's plans and purposes for your life, then you must believe that He is a good God and that He has planned a future and a hope for you.

There is a prerequisite for pregnancy that may just surprise you, but it certainly will not disqualify you. You simply have to be ordinary! Mary's story is not a fairytale where three white mice become three white horses, but Mary's story is a miracle because of the divine intervention of God! God finds joy in taking the ordinary, the mundane, and the lowly and touching it with His glory!

Luke 1 holds the beautiful story of the visitation of the angel into the world of Mary. Mary responds to the angel with heartfelt praise as she revels in the wonder of the miracle. Mary knows that she is not of high birth or privilege as she tells the angel that God has chosen to exalt the lowly. These are the words of an ordinary, poor girl from a low-class, probably uneducated family who has suddenly had the simplicity of her world invaded with hope! Her baby would be born in a barn and would have none of the comforts of children born in privilege. Nazareth, the town in which Mary was raised, was no center of spiritual promise. Mary was ordinary, but she learned that the Almighty makes Himself available to the ordinary! God loves to start with ordinary and turn it into extraordinary!

I hope that you have not considered abortion as you have waited along with Hannah, Sarah, and Elizabeth for the fulfillment of the promise. I hope that you have not given up and aborted the dream. If you have, fan the flame and bring it back to life! God takes dead things...things that are even stinking...and breathes His life back into them! The Holy Spirit tells us in Revelation 21:5 that we serve a God who makes all things new!

Perhaps it is necessary for you to pray and ask the same God who breathed life into the soul of Eve to breathe life back into that which you have aborted. He is well able to make it new again and fresh enough to fill every corner of your nursery!

***Expecting a Miracle!***

If, when you think of being pregnant, all you think of are prenatal vitamins and weight gain and Lamaze classes, then you have it all wrong.

If, when you think of the nursery of your heart, all you think of are diapers and rocking horses and rattles, then...once again...you have it all wrong.

But if, when you think of being expectant, you realize that God was willing to accept temporary housing in a womb in order to communicate His desire to use humans as His vessels through which He could change the world...then you have it all right.

The Father is still looking for women. Ordinary women - the young and the wrinkled, the sinner and the righteous, the woman with a past and the prayer warrior - through which He can change the world.

What seed has He placed within you? Have you heard His voice lately? Are you filled with grand expectation concerning your destiny? Are you anticipating His willingness to use you? Can you say with Eve...with Sarah...with Hannah...with Elizabeth...with Mary...and with me..."I'm pregnant!"

# Chapter Four

# THE WEIGHT ROOM

The word enjoyable does not describe this room. Neither does the word relaxing...or lovely...or welcoming. This room reeks of sweat, and while a short time spent in this room is productive, the longer you stay here the more you may grow to despise this place! This is the place of aching muscles, heavy breathing, profuse sweat, and profound tiredness.

Most women have a love-hate relationship with the weight room. We love the results, but we hate the process. We love the new measurements, but we hate the work that it takes to achieve the new measurements! There are slogans all over the walls of this room. This room shouts phrases like "No pain...no gain!" Or "Never, never, never give up!" Or "Winners never quit, and quitters never win!" Honestly, I am ready to throw up before I even get on the treadmill! Who said that the rooms of my heart had to include a weight room, anyway? I'll just go for a walk in the neighborhood while admiring my neighbor's flowers. A weight room? In my own home? Maybe I will redecorate; I have always wanted a craft room or a library. I'm not sure that a weight room will really get much use in my heart!

***Welcome to God's Weight Room!***

Excuses...excuses...excuses! We all have a million of them. We are able to conjure up more reasons why we should not exercise than Nike has types of shoes. The truth of the matter is that Jesus is in the weight room as distinctively as He is in the laying of the foundation, as He is in the deaths that bring us life, and as He is in the dreams and destiny of our heart. He is in it all! And so, now He is calling us to experience a new room with Him. Each room of our heart has a particular purpose and a certain goal. Nothing in our life is wasted, and certainly the time that is spent in the weight room is purposeful and productive. So, here we are! It's time to put on your sweatpants and a ratty old T-shirt. It's time to trade your high heels for running shoes and your Rolex for a stopwatch. Ladies...welcome to God's weight room!

### *Out of Control...Out of Shape...and in Denial*

What happens in every weight room in every gym in every town in America the first week of January every year? Women of all shapes and sizes sign up to join the gym or health club so that they can spend time in the weight room. Their eating habits have gotten out of control over the holidays, and so has their physique. These ladies have looked in the mirror and have exclaimed in sheer horror, "Who is that marshmallow?" Or a formerly size 10 disciplined woman has tried to zip up her size 12 slacks and has discovered that the zipper has broken! Imagine that!

Or, perhaps, for the first time since Thanksgiving turkey, Christmas eggnog, and New Year's ham, a middle-aged mom has stepped on the scale and has burst into tears at the number that appears on the dial. The weight room was made for women just like these...and for women just like you and me. God has a weight room as well, and it is for those of us who are out of control, out of shape, and in denial. It is for those of us who no longer like what we see and are learning that we have only ourselves to blame for what is in the mirror.

> Therefore we do not lose heart, but though our outer man is decaying, yet our inner man is being renewed day by day. For momentary, light affliction is producing for us an eternal weight of glory far beyond all comparison, while we look not at the things which are seen, but at the things which are not seen; for the things which are seen are temporal, but the things which are not seen are eternal. **– 2 CORINTHIANS 4:16-18**

As God's people, we are much stronger than we sometimes realize, and it is comforting to know that we can deal with the disappointments of life with the strength that He has given to us. Serving as a pastor's wife for over a quarter of a century, I have seen countless men and women of God deal with trials and tragedy beyond human endurance. But God in His omnipotence has given them the strength to place one foot in front of the other and carry on in the face of insurmountable odds.

### ***Tragedy, Trauma, and Triumph***

It was an incredible sunset - one of those paintings of purple and gold that is painted only by the Master Artist Himself. We were on our way to our son Christopher's football game, and I was captured by the glory of God shown in the mid-Atlantic sky. When we arrived at the high school football field, we were welcomed by a blaring band, a cannon that actually fired, and a crowd that was ready to send us back home! It was high school football rivalry at its finest! The home team was certainly ready to beat our boys - the reigning state champions. Our football team was known for great coaching, hard hitting, and a running offense. Our team was well-disciplined, and although they were the fiercest team in the conference, they were not allowed to play "dirty ball." Their hits were clean, and their language matched their hits.

During the second quarter of the game, the sky was still blazing in glory. After one particular play, the running back from the opposing team made a nice run, was tackled soundly, and then ran to his huddle. He looked at his coach and said, "Coach, I can't breathe." The young man then fell to the ground. We, on the opposite side of the field, didn't notice that anything was wrong until several minutes had passed, and finally one of our parents pointed out that a crowd had gathered around one of the opposing players who was on the ground. If you have ever been to a high school football game, unfortunately, this is a common occurence. Boys have the wind knocked out of them, they pull hamstrings, and sometimes high school football can even cause broken bones. One of our coaches, an emergency medical technician, ran to the other side of the field to see if he could help. When he started screaming for his medical bag and then for an ambulance, our parents started praying. From across the field, I could see a mother screaming in agony while the father was on his hands and knees on the field, rocking back and forth. Our parents started to cry and pray as our boys turned toward the stands. It was a ten minutes that lasted for eternity. The lifeless body of #32 was taken to the hospital by ambulance, but it was too late. His heart had never recovered a rhythm after he had been hit. We stayed at the school for hours with the other team, their parents, and cheerleaders. We sang "Amazing Grace" to the grieving friends and family members. We quoted scriptures in the silence of the night and then sang, "Lord, prepare me to be a sanctuary...." When the sun set that evening in September, a young man of God had gone home.

The family of the fallen player was no stranger to tragedy, having lost a baby years earlier to a heart condition. When the grieving mother arrived home in the early hours of the morning, she went to her room with only her Bible. She was in the weight room of life. This mother, touched by the deaths of two of her children, stayed in her room for thirty-six hours straight and did not come out until she had peace with God. She prayed...she cried...she yelled...she sang...she grieved...she groaned. This mother sweat and fought until she was breathless. But when she emerged, although the tears came often, she was the beneficiary of the eternal weight of glory.

The boys on our football team were invited to the funeral of the young man who was now in heaven. They solemnly dressed in their football jerseys and traveled down the same roads that only four days earlier had filled their young hearts with anticipation. Now, they were making the same journey with dread. At the church, there was reserved seating for the boys, right behind the football team of the fallen player. Our coaches received word that our team was invited to the home of the grieving parents after the funeral. As our boys stood awkwardly in the backyard where #32 had played in the sandbox and hit imaginary homeruns, his parents came out to greet our young men. The mother said, "I want to meet the boy who made the tackle." She threw her arms around the serious young man and said, "You were the last one to touch my son this side of heaven!" Because she had spent time in the weight room, she looked at the silent, young team and said, "I do not blame you for my son's death. I do not understand it, but I know that he is in heaven. I want you to play football. I want you to be happy. I do not want you to blame yourselves or blame God." This mother had learned the secret, while in the weight room, of looking at the things that were not seen. She knew that life on the football side of life was temporary, but that life on the sunset side of life was eternal. That is one of the lessons that God teaches us in the weight room.

The weight room demands of us a strenuous schedule and arduous activity, but through God's Spirit in the weight room, we experience renewal.

***The Weight of the Word***

Do you not know? Have you not heard? The everlasting God, the LORD, the Creator of the ends of the earth does not become weary or tired. His understanding is inscrutable. He gives strength to the weary, and to him who lacks might He increases power. Though youths grow weary and tired, and vigorous young men stumble badly, yet those who wait for the LORD will gain new strength; they will mount up with wings like eagles, they will run and not get tired, They will walk and not become weary. – **ISAIAH 40:28-31**

The reason that God has you in the weight room is so that He can strengthen you. He wants you to become just like Him, and He never grows weary or becomes tired! God wants to give to you that exact same strength that empowers Him! He wants you to experience His supernatural omnipotence every day that you live. When you grow weary, He gives you strength from the supply of divine strength! If all that He was giving to you was human strength, you would not need Him! But when God gives, He gives like Himself. When God gives, He gives of Himself. When you lack might and feel that you are going to faint, He gives to you throne room power! The power that He offers to you is not from a vitamin, from a self-help guru, or a natural by-product of good lineage, but when God gives power to His children, He gives power that never diminishes! You might feel as though your legs are about to collapse and your lungs about to explode, and God says, "Come with me to the weight room. I will be your personal trainer. Let me show you some exercises that will increase your capacity to deal with stress!"

The first piece of exercise equipment to which He leads you is not a large or a heavy piece of equipment. The very first piece of equipment with which you start in the weight room are the dumbbells. Weight trainers start their clients with light dumbbells and elementary exercises. Gradually, as the client gains strength, the dumbbells used are heavier and the exercises become more intense.

God has the same strategy with us in the weight room of our heart. He hands us the Bible and allows us to read one or two tender verses. When we have digested the truth and the meaning of two now familiar verses, then He leads us to deeper and richer passages. God has the intimate knowledge that it is the Word of God that will strengthen us. Psalm 37:34 says, "Wait for the LORD and keep His way." God's way is His Word, and His Word will always give us strength when we are weary and tired. Psalm 119:28 says, "My soul weeps because of grief; strengthen me according to Your word." When you are weak and are going through a time of grief, the weight room is exactly the place where you belong! God will give you strength according to the amount of time that you spend in His Word!

During the season in my life when I was grappling with the issue of infertility and was losing baby after baby after baby, the Word of God became my very lifeline to heaven! I slept with the Word of God open on my bed...I carried the Bible with me from room to room. When I was doing the dishes, I had my Bible open on the kitchen counter. When I was in the laundry room, I had my Bible open on top of the dryer. When I was playing with Legos on the floor with my boys, I had the Word of God open on the floor beside me. I was weak...I was without strength, and I knew that I was on the verge of emotional collapse. My life became the Word of God! I actually laminated 3x5 index cards with Scripture verses on them and took them in the shower with me! It worked! God strengthened me with His Word. Although I tottered on the precipice of depression, I did not fall in! My strength was found not in my ability to conceive and carry babies to full term, but my strength was found in the Word of God! I was so grateful for the weight room!

***An Extravagant Possibility***

For this reason also, since the day we heard of it, we have not ceased to pray for you and to ask that you may be filled with the knowledge of His will in all spiritual wisdom and understanding, so that you will walk in a manner worthy of the Lord, to please Him in all respects, bearing fruit in every good work and increasing in the knowledge of God; strengthened with all power, according to His glorious might, for the attaining of all steadfastness and patience; joyously giving thanks to the Father, who has qualified us to share in the inheritance of the saints in Light. – **COLOSSIANS 1:9-12**

Hang on to your water bottles, ladies! This is powerful stuff in the sweaty, stinky weight room of your heart! These verses are a prayer...a hymn. They are doctrine and deep theology. These verses should be words that are straight from the throne room of God into your heart on the treadmill of your life. H-m-m-m, the treadmill...now that sounds like fun, doesn't it? The treadmill...where the scenery never changes and it seems as if you are going absolutely nowhere. Going somewhere is not the goal of the weight room...strength is the goal in the weight room.

This prayer that Paul is praying for the church at Colossae is that they would be "filled with the knowledge of His will in all spiritual wisdom and understanding."

To be filled with something does not mean half full or "kinda–sorta" filled. If a recipe calls for a full cup, then 3/4 cup will not meet the requirements of the recipe. To be filled with the knowledge of His will means to be filled to the very top. It is God's will that you would be 100 percent assured of His will.

When reading a recipe in a cookbook, the amount is listed first and then the specific ingredient comes immediately after the amount. This verse says that the amount is "filled" and the ingredient is "the knowledge of His will." To know God's will is the battle cry of every Christian. Discerning the will of God is our earthly task – it is not easy, yet it is obvious.

Being on the treadmill in the weight room of your heart could be compared to discerning God's will for your life. The treadmill is not necessarily an easy exercise if you do it the right way. You must continuously increase the speed while at the same time increasing the incline. This is not an easy way to approach exercise, but it is obvious! You obviously know what you have to do next on the treadmill. You place one foot in front of the other and breathe!

Discerning God's will, spiritually, is the surrender of our identity as human beings. We should become more identified with Christ's kingdom than with our earthly existence. God's will is not some illusive butterfly flitting close to you, but always far enough from you so that you are not able to touch it. God's will is not that famous orange carrot in front of your nose, either, that is always one step away. You will discern God's will for your life while you are on the treadmill in the weight room of your heart.

What is God's will? One example would be that God's will for your life is to walk through cancer with the joy of the Lord! You can be sure that God's will is not necessarily a certain time, place, or date. Romans 14:17 says, "The kingdom of God is not eating and drinking, but righteousness and peace and joy in the Holy Spirit." God's will for your life is not boxed in by what you are eating or drinking or wearing. It is not determined by where you live or what your college degree enables you to do. God's will for your life is having peace in the midst of turmoil and showing forth His righteousness when everyone else is diving into compromise!

It is blasphemy against God to worry or to give in to hopelessness when we are dealing with disappointments and tragedy. We need to affirm the almightiness of God in our lives and do everything possible to authenticate our faith. We need to press on while stepping up the pace on the treadmill and not grow weary in well-doing. We need to sing while the incline increases and pray when the pain invades...then we will be authentic Christians!

After we have discerned God's will, we then need to request the power to perform His will! "So that you would walk in a manner worthy of the Lord, to please Him in all respects, bearing fruit in every good work and increasing in the knowledge of God" (Col. 1:10). Discerning God's will is only part one of the hard stuff of the weight room of your heart. After discovering God's will, then you need to ask for the power to do His will. I can guarantee you that it will require power beyond your human resources!

The first thing for which we need the power is to walk worthy and therefore to please Him in all respects. If the goal of walking worthy is sinless perfection and a continual untainted ethical performance, then I will never be able to do it! But here is some really great news: that is not what Paul is referring to in these verses from Colossians! Paul is talking about the shape and the substance of my commitment. Am I passionately eager to please God in all that I do? That is God's will for my life, and that is what I need the power to perform! Am I willing to sing through sorrow and to praise instead of whine? Am I willing to encourage instead of gossip and to believe the best about others rather than to criticize? Am I willing to love the weird...the unlovable...the irregular? Those are the types of issues that require great power from the throne room of God.

After discerning God's will, we then must remember to ask for the power to do it! When I first discern God's will through His Word and then ask Him for the power to do it, I will be a fruit-bearing Christian! My vines will be loaded and dripping in abundance! I am going to have a basket-breaking harvest of love...joy...peace...patience...kindness...self-control...goodness...and gentleness! I will have so much fruit that I will have more than enough to share with the world around me! That is God's will for my life and yours!

***Be a name-dropper! After all, you know God!***

When I am sharing the fruit of the Spirit generously with the world around me, then I truly am privy to knowledge of God that many people do not possess. I will know God and will even increase in my knowledge of God! The fact that your knowledge of God is increasing means that you are going to know Him even better as the years go by. When you know God, you must never forget the importance of being a name-dropper! Do not neglect to drop His name everywhere you go!

"Oh, by the way, sweet saleslady, did you know that I know God? I do...I know Him. We are on a first-name basis!"

"Grumpy tele-marketer, have I had the chance to tell you yet in this phone conversation that I actually know God? It's true...I meet with Him every day. He actually sets time aside on His very busy calendar just for little old me!"

"Girl who does my nails, let's talk about God today instead of Julia Roberts and Katie Couric. Did you know that I know God? He is actually my best friend. I have coffee with Him every day, and He is never too busy or too important to spend time with me."

The next verse, verse 11, is my very favorite in all of Colossians. This says that once we have discerned the will of God and then asked for the power to perform His will, He will strengthen us with all of His power! God has a power source in heaven, and when you need power or strength, He does not dole it out in small amounts! Our generous heavenly Father would not know how to give something in tiny amounts if He tried! There is only one way that He gives, and that is lavishly! When you need strength, He gives you all that He has! His power is available to you in any situation during any season of your life. God has strength in heaven with your name written on it. If you are a young mother, He has strength for you to get through sleepless nights and through the teachable twos! If you are a single mother, He has strength for you to build rockets and to go on campouts with your rambunctious boys! If you are a single woman, He has strength to get you through the loveless holidays and the lonely nights. If you are a widow, He has the strength to give you every day of every year! If you need God's strength and power, it's only a prayer away!

One translation of Colossians 1:11 says that we will be "strengthened with strength of every kind." So, not only does God give you all that He has, but also He has strengths of different kind at your instant disposal. When do you need strength? When do you need power? When do you feel the weakest? At a certain time of the month? God has strength with your name on it during every day of every month! Do you need strength when the children are cross?

Here it comes...the strength that every mother needs in dealing with cantankerous children! Do you need strength on the days that you pay the bills? He has that strength that is set aside for you in your time of need! Maybe you need strength because someone has hurt your feelings...it's on its way special delivery to the front door of your heart! God has strength for all of that and even more! God has strength of every kind in His storehouse in heaven. He has strength with the word "cancer" stamped across the front. He has strength for disappointment, divorce, and tragedy.

When God gives us this strength, He gives according to the might of His glory! What an extravagant possibility! When God gives strength to you as you are going through the sudden death of a loved one, God gives you strength in proportion to the might of His glory! You are going to be strengthened in mighty, supernatural ways and be filled with His glory just when you need it the most! You will have the exact same strength that David was given when he faced the giant Goliath! God will give to you the same power and might that he gave to Esther as she walked uninvited into the throne room of a very angry king! God will give to you the same strength that He gave to Jesus when Jesus was in utter and absolute pain on the cross of Calvary.

The reason that we need to be strengthened with strength of every kind according to His glorious might is for the attaining of steadfastness and patience! When hard things come into your life, you will be a steadfast and a patient Christian. The characteristic of steadfastness is the refusal to be daunted by hard times. If you are a patient Christian, you will refuse to be upset by perverse people. You will no longer lose your breath as you contemplate bill-paying Friday! His strength will meet your most intimate needs. You will no longer be weak in the knees at the thought of spending time with your mother-in-law! You will look forward to every holiday because you have been strengthened with God! You will be like a tree planted by a water supply whose roots go deep into the rich, moist earth, and you will not be moved!

After the excitement and anticipation that was birthed in your heart in the nursery, God stabilizes and strengthens you with the time spent in the weight room. When you walk out of the door of the nursery, you are pumped and ready to take on the world! Your heart is filled with the possibility of new dreams and God's purposes on this world being accomplished through you! Imagine that! As you left the nursery with your adrenalin flowing and more vision than you ever thought possible, God led you into a time of waiting. The purpose of the weight room is that you would be strengthened for everything that God has for you. If you left the nursery and went straight into your destiny, you would be weak and incapable of completing the task. Your outlook would be that of a novice, and although your heart would be filled with good intentions, your experience would be sadly lacking. God placed you in the weight room to strengthen and empower you so that you would have His perspective of eternity. God's plans for your life do not come with an expiration date attached. They come with eternity in mind! If you spend enough time in the weight room, His strength will be made perfect in you.

> And He has said to me, "My grace is sufficient for you, for power is perfected in weakness." Most gladly, therefore, I will rather boast about my weaknesses, so that the power of Christ may dwell in me. Therefore I am well content with weaknesses, with insults, with distresses, with persecutions, with difficulties,

for Christ's sake; for when I am weak, then I am strong.
**– 2 CORINTHIANS 12:9-10**

We go into the Weight Room looking like a weakling with no muscle tone, no lung capacity, and no endurance at all, but we exit the weight room being fit for His service, because in our weakness, He has made us strong!

# Chapter Five

# THE KITCHEN

"Supper is ready! Come and get it!"

"Mom! I can't find my history book! Do you know where it is?"

"Son, it's time to get off the computer."

"Has anyone seen the cat?"

"Mom! Telephone is for you!"

"No, I'm sorry, but the first week in April is not good for me. Is there another possibility?"

"We are so glad that you were able to come over for dinner. What a blessing to have you here!"

I love the sounds of my kitchen! There are other rooms that I only tolerate, like the laundry room...or those bathrooms. But now, my kitchen...I could live my entire life in that one room. There is always something cooking in the kitchen...always a party ready to happen! A kitchen is where a woman spends a large portion of her life. Historians claim that from the early 1600s until 1940, a woman spent 90 percent of her life in two places: her kitchen and her kitchen garden.

The reason that my kitchen holds such a special place in my heart is because the hours spent there are such happy ones. In my kitchen, I cook for the people whom I love the very most in the whole entire universe! I plan menus, cut recipes and coupons, and pray as I do the dishes in my kitchen. I am on the phone, on the computer, and in my motherly element in the kitchen. The coffee pot is always brewing, and my Bible is always open. The kitchen is where I have the hardest time with discipline...so often what I place in my mouth consumes me! It is here that we play those riotous, competitive games with the family. You have not lived until you have played our own raucous family game we call "Mow" in the McLeod family kitchen! Children do schoolwork, pets are underfoot, the phone is ringing...the kitchen is full of life! This is where Craig and I have our heart-to-heart talks and where we pray for our children. We entertain in the kitchen because the dining room is too formal. The kitchen in our house seems to sing, "Welcome home!"

Unfortunately, the kitchen is also the busiest room in the house. If there is clutter, it shows up in the kitchen. If there is a mess, it finds its way to the kitchen counter. Stacks of paper, books, games, mail, and lists have converged into one great mountain on my kitchen table, ready to erupt at any moment! If there is noise, confusion, or activity, it is in here. There is always a child wanting to talk or wanting food. I keep my calendar in there. It is well hidden behind the pantry door, but my calendar is a cacophony of people wanting a piece of my time. Why do I do this to myself?

The kitchen of your heart is the busiest room in your heart. It is time to clear out the clutter and make room for the Lord's purposes and presence in the kitchen of your heart.

***The Barrenness of Busyness***

My mother-in-law recently told me that she had read a story of Anne Graham Lotz, the daughter of Billy and Ruth Graham, who is a respected Bible teacher and author. Anne calls her mother often to check on her because Ruth is elderly and her health has been fragile for sometime. Anne calls her mother from wherever she is on the road just so that her mother can hear her voice. During one particular phone conversation, Anne was reciting all that she needed to do, the places that she was speaking, the television shows on which she would be appearing, and the books that she was writing. Ruth, who apparently has grown quiet as she has become older, broke into Anne's litany of "things to do and people to see" and suddenly exhorted, "Beware the barrenness of busyness!" What a word for our generation! What a word for me!

With more appliances and creature comforts, with more money to spend on vacations and time away from it all, we remain the busiest generation in history EVER! Is that really the legacy we desire to pass to our children and our grandchildren? It is quite easy and uncomplicated to explain why our generation is the busiest in all of recorded history. The reason that we are breathless, worn-out, fed-up, and overcommitted is due to the fact that we have chosen it to be so. It is our choice to be busy and to stay busy. You have no one to blame for your schedule but yourself. It is just as easy to say "No!" as it is to say "Yes!" It is a matter of setting priorities and then sticking to them. Life is seasonal, and a woman must make choices consistent with her season in life in order to fulfill her destiny and purposes.

I must confess that I have always chosen to be a busy person, and nearly every day of my existence, I am not proud of this choice. I will never forget the day, during my senior year in college, when I was buzzing across campus at 7:00 a.m. I was trying to complete three majors, taking 24 credit hours, was newly engaged, and was writing my senior paper. I was a dorm director and was accompanying five senior recitals along with the concert choir. I was speaking in Vespers that week and had a deadline for the student newspaper. As I dashed across campus early one morning, I providentially ran into the head of the campus counseling center. Because I did not have time for an appointment with this wise woman, I tearfully asked her on the run, "Will my life always be like this?"

"Yes," she said as she placed her arms around me, "your life will always be like this because life is about the choices that you make, and this is who you are. Only you can decide if you want to be this busy or not. It is up to you."

Her words were indelibly written on my soul that spring morning in Oklahoma. I have never forgotten the life principle that my life is a reflection of my choices. I do not want to be the busiest mom on the street, nor do I want to have an agenda that is compiled by other people's demands. I want to hear His voice clearly and follow His plan every day of my life. The sad commentary is that for most of my life I did not even have time to hear His voice.

### *The Heart of Hospitality*

> Now as they were traveling along, He entered a village; and a woman named Martha welcomed Him into her home. She had a sister called Mary, who was seated at the Lord's feet, listening to His word. But Martha was distracted with all her preparations; and she came up to Him and said, "Lord, do You not care that my sister has left me to do all the serving alone? Then tell her to help me." But the Lord answered and said to her, "Martha, Martha, you are worried and bothered about so many things; but only one thing is necessary, for Mary has chosen the good part, which shall not be taken away from her." – **LUKE 10:38-42**

Mary and Martha are symbolic of two different types of women, not one good and one bad...just different. Some of us are Martha's, some of us are Mary's, but most of us are a combination of the two. There is room for different personality types in the body of Christ, and we should never force anyone into our personality mold; Jesus made us just the way we are for a reason. It is His divine pleasure to revel in our differences and yet love us all just the same. This principle does not give us the excuse to stay the way we are and to wallow in our weaknesses, but it does challenge us not to judge others!

Mary and Martha are forever bound together in Scripture like Cain and Abel, Jacob and Esau, and Jonathan and David. They are bound together not just because they were sisters but because of the hospitality that they showed to Jesus and because of their love for Jesus. Mary and Martha were distinctly different sisters though raised in the same home. Martha was the doer and the achiever of the family with her first-century type-A personality! Mary, on the other hand, would have been completely content living in a convent because she was the mediator, the worshiper, and she tended to be introspective.

We can presume that Martha was the elder sister in the home because she seemed to take self-worth from the fact that she was in charge. Martha was a leader, an administrator, and a woman who was perfectly capable of getting the job done all by her self. I do believe that Martha deserves a bit of defending here, however. I believe that history has been hard on Martha, and I would like to point out some issues from her perspective.

Can you imagine thirteen dirty, sweaty, and hungry men dropping by for supper one evening? There was no phone call giving advance notice or an e-mail detailing the time of arrival. Perhaps there was a messenger boy sent on ahead by thirty minutes or so, but that was the only notice that Martha had. These men who were coming to dine at Martha's table had not showered in days. Their antiperspirant soap had worn off days earlier, along with all vestiges of a long-lasting deodorant. These men did not don clean garments just prior to walking into Martha's pristine door. Can you imagine twenty-six feet walking in your door that had been covered with only the barest of sandals? Feet that had been walking through dust, dirt, and animal excrement for many days? These feet alone would make most high school locker rooms smell springtime fresh!

But, the Bible tells us that "Martha welcomed Him." Martha extended her hospitality to these men and treated them just as if the king and his entourage had arrived. Romans 12:13 exhorts men and women from all centuries and all cultures to practice hospitality. The word *practice* is the keyword in this phrase, which means to rehearse it over and over and over. Do you have time to practice hospitality, or is your calendar so booked with soccer games, ballet lessons, meetings, and appointments that the first time you could have someone in your home is three months from now? Having the pastor and his wife over for dinner in January does not fill your hospitality quotient for the year. You must practice it. Whether you live in a high-rise apartment building, a farmhouse with a white picket fence, or a handyman's special, this verse is for you. You are not disqualified from practicing hospitality due to your schedule or your living situation.

Practicing hospitality is not just for happily married women, either. Single women should make it a point to open their homes as often as possible to families with children, college students, missionaries home on furlough, and people that they meet on the job. Hospitality is not about pretense, but it is about presence.

Hospitality is, quite simply put, sharing the love of Christ that resides in your home with the world around you.

Do not neglect to show hospitality to strangers, for by this some have entertained angels without knowing it! – **HEBREWS 13:2**

Many of us have been disobedient to this New Testament scripture our entire adult life without even realizing it. We barely have our own family over to dinner. Who has time for neighbors and people I don't even know? Not in this decade! But this scripture offers a blessing that if we do not neglect having strangers in our home, we might just be entertaining angels who have worshiped in the presence of God!

One of the main purposes for the kitchen of your heart is described in this verse from Hebrews. If you are neglecting hospitality, then you are neglecting your kitchen as well. Hospitality should not add busyness to your life, but it should give purpose to your life. Your kitchen is where you reach out to others, it is where you give of yourself, and it is where you bring the world into your home. You do not have to go on the mission field...your life is a mission field! There is a lost and dying world just outside your front door, and you have the power to invite them in and share with them the presence of Jesus in your home. Start by inviting your neighbors, the woman whom you see walking every morning with her dog, your children's teachers, the people with whom you work and their families. That list alone will keep you busy for the first year or two at least!

I have found that many twenty-first-century women are totally turned off by what they presume to be a 1950s mind-set that the little wife has on an apron and a string of pearls after cleaning all day and is absolutely thrilled to have her husband's boss in for dinner. If that is the picture that you think I have painted, go back to the beginning of the chapter and read it again! When I have guests in my home, rarely has my living room been dusted or my floor washed. I have given the bathroom a quick once-over so my guests are not totally grossed out by the way we live! I might order pizza and wings or throw together a simmering pot of soup. I have two or three easy company menus that I fix time after time. My children get tired of the company menus, but the visitors do not; they don't know that it is the third time this month that I have served the exact same menu! Dessert is always McLeod-cookies made by my thirteen-year-old daughter and whatever ice cream is on sale that week. When you light a candle and play some great worship music, you have a lovely evening filled with new friends just waiting to be loved by you and by Jesus!

I know many women who have the consummate gift of hospitality. Recently we had dinner with a family whom we love dearly, and I could easily be intimidated by their lifestyle if I kept my eyes on people rather than on Jesus. The evening started with everyone making a craft together that would adorn the center of the dining room table as we ate. Then, as the mother placed a lovely dinner on the table, the girls made trays of food to take to their elderly neighbors. We had a delicious homemade dinner by candlelight and then ate the dessert that I had *bought* on the way to their house because I was too busy to bake! After dinner, the girls brewed all kinds of herb teas for us as we retired to the living room for an evening of conversation. Their girls taught my girls how to knit and how to make dolls while the mother showed me the rug that she was making as a wedding gift! I realized after that wonderful evening that I do not have their gift, but Jesus still calls me to show hospitality!

You, like me, may not have the gift of hospitality the way that my lovely friends have cultivated the gift, but you and I can still practice hospitality until we become very proficient at it! What I have learned from my friends is that you are not successful at hospitality when you serve a seven-course meal, use linen tablecloths, and have Chopin playing in the background. However, you have learned the secret of hospitality when you share your heart, your home, and your love for Jesus with the world around you.

***Cluttered Emotions***

> "For I was hungry, and you gave Me something to eat; I was thirsty and you gave Me something to drink; I was a stranger and you invited Me in; naked and you clothed Me; I was sick, and you visited Me; I was in prison, and you came to Me." Then the righteous will answer Him, "Lord, when did we see You hungry, and feed You, or thirsty, and give You something to drink? And when did we see You a stranger, and invite You in, or naked, and clothe You? When did we see You sick, or in prison, and come to You?" The King will answer and say to them, "Truly I say to you, to the extent that you did it to one of these brothers of Mine, even the least of them, you did it to Me." **– MATTHEW 25:35-40**

These verses from the Book of Matthew describe our historical sister Martha. Do these verses describe you as well? Martha had the opportunity to show hospitality to our Lord and Savior, and she gave it her best. Martha did have one problem, however. Martha's problem was not her actions, but it was her attitude. Martha was doing the right thing with the wrong motivation. Martha did not have a happy heart.

> But Martha was distracted with all her preparations; and she came up to Him and said, "Lord, do You not care that my sister has left me to do all the serving alone? Then tell her to help me." – **LUKE 10:40**

Martha was distracted and anxious; one translation of the Bible says that she was worried and bothered. Quite frankly, Martha was frustrated with a capital "F" and was struggling with an attitude that is common among women when they feel that they have been taken advantage of. Martha was allowing her emotions to rule her spirit, which is a tormenting problem for many Christian women. What Martha was *doing* became more important than who she *was*. Martha found her value not in her Savior but in her service to the Savior. And so, as women have through all of recorded history, Martha started to whine! She took her frustration out on the Lord! When we are too busy and overcommitted, what is truly in our hearts is revealed, and Martha becomes an open book in this verse. Martha said, "Lord, do You not care?" Martha was accusing the Lord, whose very existence is defined by the word love, of not caring. My heart is in my throat...surely Martha wanted to take the words back...longed to push the rewind button.

Have you ever done that? Have you accused the Lord of not caring about your life? When I get too busy...when what I am doing becomes more important than who I am...when I allow others to frustrate me...I will say things to the Lord that I have no business saying. When I reach this point in my busyness, I realize that once again, I have allowed my emotions to rule my spirit. Martha accused

Him of not caring simply due to the unhealthy fact that her preparations had taken precedence and because she was frustrated with her sister. I have been haunted for those exact same reasons. I get so busy that my eyes are on people, not on His presence in my life, and then I take my frustration out on Him! I can hardly believe that I have allowed my life choices to drive me to such a heartbreaking place. "Lord! Help me with my clutter!"

There is a verse from Ecclesiastes 5 that has revolutionized my conversational life with the Lord. This verse says that we should not be hasty or impulsive to bring up a matter in the presence of God. It reminds us of the very clear fact that God is in heaven and we are only on earth. This verse exhorts us to let our words be few in the presence of God. My tongue needs to be reminded that I do not get to say everything I think, feel, and believe when I am in the presence of God! I must enter His presence with reverence and the ever present knowledge that He is God...and I am not. (See Ecclesiastes 5:2.)

### *The Heart of the Issue*

> She had a sister called Mary, who was seated at the Lord's feet, listening to His word. **– LUKE 10:39**

Mary was presumably the younger sister who had allowed Martha to take the lead role in the home. Mary was seated at the Lord's feet, listening to His words and drinking in His presence! Martha was preparing a feast while Mary was feasting at the feet of Jesus. Mary was hungry and thirsty, but not for the banquet meal that Martha was preparing. Mary was being filled to overflowing by just resting in the presence of the One that she knew as "Teacher." Matthew 4:4 declares, "Man shall not live on bread alone but on every word that proceeds out of the mouth of God."

Mary knew well that the things of this earth were not satisfactory to her and that the only thing that would truly satisfy her inner hunger was to sit at the feet of Jesus. In so many ways I am a Martha, but it is at the feet of Jesus that Mary and I are kindred spirits though separated by two millennia of living. When I am in His presence, basking in the peace of who He is, I once again find myself and who I was created to be. Nothing satisfies my hungry soul like time spent at His feet, bowing to His authority and worshiping with every drop of energy that my soul can muster.

> But whoever drinks of the water that I will give him shall never thirst. – **JOHN 4:14**

Mary knew that at the end of the meal, in a few short hours the process would begin again with more cleaning, more preparation and cooking, and more devouring of only temporary fare regardless of how delectable it might be. Mary had her priorities straight and did not desire to merely prepare physical food for her Lord, but she wanted to partake of His spiritual food. When we find more value in serving the Lord than in spending time at His feet, we will need an attitude readjustment just as Martha did. But when, like Mary, we find value and satisfaction in savoring His presence, we have begun to clear out the clutter in the kitchen of our hearts.

> But the Lord answered and said to her, "Martha, Martha, you are worried and bothered about so many things; but only one thing is necessary, for Mary has chosen the good part, which shall not be taken away from her." – **LUKE 10:41-42**

Jesus answered Martha in love (it is, by the way, the only way that He knows how to answer) and went straight to the heart of her issue. When we whine, He responds by speaking the truth in love. He is, after all, Love, and it is His only possible response. Will you allow Jesus to go to the heart of your issues? Jesus neither agreed nor disagreed with Martha's point of view; neither did Jesus address Mary and ask her to help her sister, because this was not Mary's problem; it was Martha's problem. Martha wanted Jesus to fix her situation and change the circumstances. It has been my experience that Jesus rarely "fixes" my situation; He usually "fixes" me instead. Jesus is not as concerned about my circumstances as He is about my issues. Many times when I cry out to God in my frustration, when I question whether He really cares about what is going on in my life, when I accuse someone else of contributing to my frustration, He goes straight into my heart and touches my clutter with His peace. As I relax in His presence and sit at His feet, I am once again filled up with the satisfaction that only He can bring.

Jesus reminded Martha that in life, only a few things are necessary, really only one. The one thing that is necessary to live is an intimate relationship with Jesus. The only thing that is really necessary for you to be satisfied is time at His feet, drinking in His Word.

### *Primary Issues vs. Secondary Issues*

What are the few other things that are necessary in your life? The necessary things for me have always been quantity time with my family and husband. The women's movement has lied to us by saying that it is "quality time not quantity that goes into raising emotionally healthy children." Love to a child is spelled T-I-M-E, and spending hours with your husband and children should be your number one priority. For single women, the priority may be taking care of aging parents, baby-sitting nieces and nephews, or being the force that plans the annual family reunion. Do not let your singleness be an excuse for busyness. One of my favorite people in the whole world is a career single woman who has a high-power job at a national bank. She spends every Friday night during football season - whether it is raining or snowing, whether the game is at home or hours away - at her nephew's football games. She knows all of the players' names and numbers, she knows their families and their siblings' names, and she can quote statistics like a pro. When she is traveling, she buys postcards of the state university's football stadium and sends it to her nephew with the words, "You might be playing here in a couple of years. I will be there cheering for you."

Another one of the few necessary things in your life should be a commitment to your church. As a pastor's wife, I believe that if every member of the church committed to doing just one thing very well, the needs of the church would largely be met. Instead of being at church every night of the week and all day Saturday, it is time for you to pray and discern what God would have you commit yourself to within your local body of believers. When you have decided, after time in prayer, what your calling is, do that one thing with your whole heart! Be faithful in your commitment. But always remember that few things are necessary, really only one!

What else is necessary in your life? This is a dangerous question, because all of us can justify a multitude of activities: income, exercise, outreach, children's activities, shopping, errands, cleaning, yard work, paying the bills, correspondence, friends, meetings, dental and doctor appointments...I am tired and overwhelmed already! As you clean out the clutter of busyness in the kitchen of your heart, remember not to mix the primary issues and the secondary issues of your life. I know a family who has eight children, and the parents have made a conscious decision to allow their children to only participate in one activity per year. If a certain child chooses piano lessons, that means that this particular child will not play soccer, take karate, or participate in an after-school activity. If a different child is elected to a class officer position, then that child must take a break from the basketball team, church choir, and Boy Scouts. You might think that this is a ridiculous strategy in trying to clear the family's schedule, but before you jump to your twenty-first-century conclusion, allow me to say this: It is working! The children are healthy, well-behaved, and talented. They get good grades in school, have plenty of family time, and are not being eternally warped by their parents' decision to use wisdom rather than reckless abandon.

For single women, the issue of scheduling activities and community service may actually be even a more difficult issue to discern. You are in a season in your life when you do have time to give to family, the church, and your community. It is still imperative that you make your choices based upon the primary issues of your life, not upon the secondary issues. Do not fill your life with busyness, but fill your time with activities and commitments that will make a difference not only in your life but also in the lives of others. If you choose to enroll in a weekly ceramics class, it only becomes valuable from an eternal perspective if you are building relationships, reaching out to the others in your class, and sharing the love of Jesus with them. I believe that it is extremely important for single women to fill at least one corner of their heart with children. Children will keep you young and unselfish and will give you a worldview that will refresh and inspire you. Allow me to encourage all types of single women to volunteer to work in the nursery or teach the middle-school girls' Sunday school class. We all must be proactive in using our lives for eternal purposes and values, and this does not exclude unmarried women.

Whether you are single or married, have children or are childless, live near family or miles from home, reside in a Rockwellian small town or an urban jungle, the principle remains the same: Choose to invest yourself in activities that cultivate a ministry, and do not clutter the kitchen of your heart. Make your choices based on the primary issues of your life rather than the secondary issues. And remember the words of Jesus to a type-A woman from another period in history: "Few things are necessary...really only one!"

### ***Service With a Smile***

> Jesus, therefore, six days before the Passover, came to Bethany where Lazarus was, whom Jesus had raised from the dead. So they made Him a supper there, and Martha was serving, but Lazarus was one of those reclining at the table with Him. Mary then took a pound of very costly perfume of pure nard, and anointed the feet of Jesus and wiped His feet with her hair; and the house was filled with the fragrance of the perfume.
>
> **– JOHN 12:1-3, EMPHASIS ADDED**

Martha is found serving the Lord in these verses – she is still the leader, still in charge of the home, still walking in her gifts – but this time she is not busy, distracted, worried, or bothered. She is not whining or accusing the Lord of not caring – she is serving. She is not fixated on all of her preparations - she is serving. She is not distracted or frustrated – she is serving. When Jesus spoke to the issues of Martha's heart, she listened to His admonition and changed her heart motivation. Maybe it was of Martha that Jesus spoke when He said, "Whoever wishes to become great among you shall be your servant..." (Matt. 20:26). If you want to be great in God's kingdom, learn to be a servant! Your kitchen should not be known for its clutter but for its service.

"They made Him a supper there... (John 12:2). The pronoun "they" means that more than one person made the supper. I would like to think that this third person plural pronoun refers to Martha and her sister, Mary. I believe that Mary participated in the work and was a blessing to her sister in the practice of hospitality in this home. Remember, the problem was not in Martha's actions; it was in her attitudes, and the problem seems to have righted itself in this first-century home. They made Him a supper together, then Martha served, and finally, what was Mary's next action?

> Mary then took a pound of very costly perfume of pure nard and anointed the feet of Jesus and wiped His feet with her hair; and the house was filled with the fragrance of the perfume.
> **– JOHN 12:3**

After she made dinner, Mary is once again at the feet of Jesus, her favorite place in the whole world! I have found it to be my favorite place as well...what about you? Will you join Mary and me at the feet of Jesus? We have seen Mary at the feet of Jesus in worship and wonder, thirsting and hungering for wisdom. Now, we see Mary there, ministering to Jesus and anointing His body. It was a beautiful act that Mary was performing, filled with heartfelt surrender and holy giving. This particular event happened just six days before Passover when the life of Jesus on earth would end in one cataclysmic event. Mary was anointing the body of Jesus with nard, which was an embalming oil used at funerals. Perhaps Mary did not even realize what she was doing, but it was a foreshadowing of what lay ahead in the life of Jesus. The amount of nard in the jar represented the average wage of a family for an entire year! When I understand the magnitude of the gift that she was bestowing upon the One that she loved so dearly, I must stop and ask myself, "When was the last time, in the midst of my busyness, that I truly gave something to Jesus? When was the last time that, in the midst of twenty-first-century insanity, I sacrificed something holy and beautiful unto my Lord?" Like Martha, I long to serve Him well and with passion, but like Mary, I long to stay lost in His presence, at His feet, giving to Him no matter the cost.

### *Every Martha Needs a Mary*

> What use is it, my brethren, if someone says he has faith but he has no works? Can that faith save him? If a brother or sister is without clothing and in need of daily food, and one of you says to them, "Go in peace, be warmed and be filled," and yet you do not give them what is necessary for their body, what use is that? Even so faith, if it has no works, is dead, being by itself. But someone may well say, "You have faith and I have works; show me your faith without the works, and I will show you my faith by my works." You believe that God is one. You do well; the demons also believe, and shudder. But are you willing to recognize, you foolish fellow, that faith without works is useless?
> **– JAMES 2:14-20**

In Scripture, faith and deeds are intimately woven together. Every Mary needs a Martha to lead her into areas of service and giving to the body of Christ on a practical level. Conversely, Martha needs the input of a Mary to speak to her heart and help her to find her worth and value not in the actions but in the heart attitude.

In the midst of ballgames, business meetings, shopping, appointments, travel, the demands of family and friends, and even your church, allow me to ask you this hard question that is the same today as it was when Mary and Martha were confronting their life issues: Have you any room for Jesus? You have made Him Lord and Savior; now sit down with Him, in the kitchen of your heart, and have a cup of coffee together. Study the Word with Him and have a heartfelt conversation. Make room for Jesus in your life...I can guarantee you that He is sitting there at the kitchen table, observing while you rush around trying to live your life successfully. But He is sitting there...waiting for you to take a breath, turn around, and sit with Him. You will love your time spent in His presence because He will breathe new life into your demanding schedule. He will neutralize the acidity of your busyness and cause you to find purpose and significance in His presence.

Hosea 13:3 says that our lives are like the dew on the morning grass...like smoke from a chimney...like a morning cloud upon the mountain that lingers not. How will you spend your life? As the women of God in this generation, we must be very careful how we spend our time and be poignantly aware of the things in which we are investing our lives. If we stay too busy and too frustrated, we will take it out on the people we love the most and know the best. If we remain as slaves to our culture and the expectations of a world consumed with "busier is better," then we will say things to God that will reflect the devastation of a schedule out of control. It is time to clean up our kitchens and throw away the clutter. On a practical level, what are some of the things that you can let go of in order to make room for the few necessary things to which you have been called? Make a list today...ask the Lord for wisdom and guidance as you remove the litter from your life.

I have a dear friend whose husband has served in the military reserves their entire married life. Jim and Dawn have made it their heartfelt goal to build a life of significance with their three growing children. When reserve units began to be called up to go to Iraq, Jim's name was at the top of the list. He has been back and forth between the Middle East and his military base for nearly three years. When he is in the States, he is stationed at a base only two hours from home. This family made the decision that it was more important to be with Dad when he was in the States then to stay enrolled in activities, events, and pleasures. So, Dawn has gracefully said no to piano lessons, choir, basketball, and many other activities in exchange for family games played in a cramped military apartment. They have taken long walks on the beach, eaten meals together, and have looked forward with great anticipation to evenings with Dad. We may all take a lesson from this family who knows the meaning of the word "priority."

### *Older but Not Wiser*

Although it may be hard to believe, there are women who might be at different spots in their lives. The kitchen of your heart may be spotlessly clean and void of life. The counter may be immaculate with not one thing on it or on the calendar and without one morsel cooking in the oven. You might be bored with life and lonely beyond words. You may be wasting your life away not in a conundrum of activity but in a vacuum of boredom. Busy people use their time more effectively than people who are bored, and you may be whittling away the days of an unproductive life. The problem is different...but the issue is the same. An empty life sometimes is the problem for women who are widowed or retired. Please do not fill your days with television game shows, crossword puzzles, and lonely moments looking through old picture albums. Give God your calendar. Maybe you do not even own a calendar because it has not been a necessary purchase in the last ten years or so! Go buy a calendar, and then give it to God! Ask Him to fill your days with meaning and purpose. Ask God with what or with whom you should fill your life. I believe that God will show you people whom you should invite to dinner, volunteer activities that will add joy to your life, or a Bible study that will provide fellowship and stability. I believe that God is capable of whispering directions to you: "Why don't you bake some cookies for that new family down the street?" "Have you noticed the woman two doors down who takes out the trash alone...retrieves the mail alone...always drives away alone? Why don't you befriend her? She might like to go to Bible study with you." Actually schedule in time every day for prayer, reading the Word, listening to praise and worship music, and for hospitality! Your hours will soon become filled with laughter instead of loneliness and with destiny rather than desolation!

***The Blessing of Desire***

The kitchen of our heart was intended to be the place of hungering and thirsting for His presence, not a room that becomes a hodge-podge of a disarray and mess.

> Blessed are those who hunger and thirst for righteousness, for they shall be satisfied. – **MATTHEW 5:6**

I have learned that busyness is like saltwater to my thirst for Jesus. Busyness will never satisfy; it will only torture my unquenchable condition. There are blessings that are attached to every beatitude. Did you know that every blessing has a string attached? You will be blessed if you hunger and thirst after the righteousness of God. How comforting to realize that the blessing is not in the achievement of righteousness but in the hungering and in the thirsting for it! We are blessed not when we achieve goodness but when we ache for it with our whole heart! God does not bless us for our achievements but for what is in our hearts! God's love for you is not based on your performance, but it is based on the delightful pleasure that He obtains just from enjoying your heart!

> But the LORD said to my father David, "Because it was in your heart to build a house for My name, you did well that it was in your heart." – **1 KINGS 8:18**

These are the words of David's son Solomon to the people after the ark has been brought into the newly built temple. God had first spoken to David about building the temple for His name, yet David had not been the one to build or to complete the building of the house of the Lord. But God blessed David not for the building of the temple, but He blessed David because David desired to build the temple.

God will bless you as well when your desires are to please Him with your choices and with your heart attitudes. You may never attain that perfect schedule or a kitchen free from the jumble and mishmash of choices gone awry, but if you are hungering and thirsting for doing life God's way and not your own, then you will experience His pleasure in the kitchen of your heart!

> If anyone is thirsty, let him come to Me and drink.
> – **JOHN 7:37**

You will get that which you hunger and thirst for - the treasures of earth will not satisfy, and busyness will only bring out the worst in you. It is the treasures of heaven that will satisfy, because those are the primary issues of our life even here on earth. Jesus knew that neither the demands of a busy schedule nor the loneliness of a solitary existence would bring satisfaction. He came to earth and emptied Himself so that you could drink and be satisfied.

> But store up for yourselves treasures in heaven, where neither moth nor rust destroys, and where thieves do not break in or steal; for where your treasure is, there your heart will be also....But seek first His kingdom and His righteousness, and all these things will be added to you.
>
> – **MATTHEW 6:20-21, 33**

*Chapter Six*

# THE DINING ROOM

Our first Thanksgiving as newlyweds! I couldn't wait to impress my new husband with all of the secret family recipes that had been in our family for generations! Thanksgiving has always been the most important holiday of the year in my family, and I longed for the importance of this first shared significant holiday to nestle itself right into my handsome husband's heart!

I did what any novice bride would do and placed a phone call to my mother about a week before the feast day arrived. I had my paper and pencil ready along with a list of Burton-Boyce family recipes with which I couldn't wait to impress my husband!

"Mom, how do you make cranberry relish? You know, the one that Grandma Blew always used to make?"'

"Honey, you buy a bag of cranberries from the grocery store and the recipe is printed right on the back."

"How easy is that?" I thought smugly. Next question...

"Mom, what about the dressing for the turkey? I just love Dad's recipe. I know that I have watched him make it for twenty-two years, but could you give me his recipe?"

"Sure, honey. Just go to the grocery store and buy a package of dried breadcrumbs. Right on the back of the package you will find the best recipe that we have ever used for stuffing."

"Oh," I said thoughtfully. "I was sure Dad had created that recipe."

"No," replied my mother. "We have used the recipe on the back of the package for as long as I can remember."

"Mom, Craig just loves pumpkin pie. Do you have your recipe cards handy? I want your recipe for pumpkin pie. It is always so rich and moist."

"Carol, just go to the grocery store and buy a big can of pumpkin filling. You follow the recipe (you guessed it!) on the back of the can."

"MOM! Don't we have any secret family recipes?"

"Yes...the one secret recipe that we have is for Aunt Jeris' chip dip. That's one package of cream cheese, one tablespoon of mayonnaise, and some dry onion flakes."

"That's all? That's the extent of our secret family recipes for generation upon generation? Surely all of you women have something more to give me than that?"

"Sorry, honey. You really don't come from a line of great cooks. But I know that you will do just fine!"

The morning of my first Thanksgiving as a McLeod dawned bright and sunny. I cooked and baked myself into a kitchened frenzy! Our little apartment was filled to overflowing with students from the university who thought that my culinary expertise was extraordinary. (After all, they were only comparing it to college cafeteria food. Anyone could be impressive in the face of that competition!) Whenever one of the hungry, homesick students would generously compliment one of my dishes, I would smile back into their eyes and say with controlled glee, "Thank you so much. It is a secret family recipe."

### *The Legacy of the Dining Room*

"The dining room"...surely your feminine mind and heart travel to memories dearly held of lovely family get-togethers, or perhaps the snapshot that flickers into the photo album of your mind is one of holiday tables laden with culinary abundance! Possibly you picture the three times a year that your fine china is complemented with a meal that would make even your mother-in-law proud, or maybe you fondly remember generations of family basking in the joy of one another's presence. Possibly the words dining room conjure up sleek dinners with business associates and catered food that you have hurriedly placed into dishes recently purchased at Eddie Bauer! Or maybe your dining room is really your kitchen all cleaned and sparkling, and instead of slinging placemats around the table, you carefully unfold your grandmother's tablecloth that will complement the china that you bought at a yard sale three years ago!

The images are all different, but the memories are commonly shared by everyone who has spent time around a table, looking into one another's eyes and heart and knowing that life doesn't get any better than this. Whether it was a birthday celebration complete with cake and candles, a fully stuffed turkey at Thanksgiving that was topped off by pumpkin pie, or a pristine dinner party with business associates, the dining room is a place of fellowship, relationship, and the promise of another meal shared with those we love the most and know the best.

### *The South Shall Rise Again*

Our first Thanksgiving living in North Carolina was especially memorable because we were combining my Yankee heritage and the

Southern hospitality of Craig's family for the very first time. We were living in a new home and were excited about sharing this day with his side of the family, who had lived in North Carolina for over one hundred years, and my side of the family, who had just moved south after living in western New York for as many generations as we could remember. Our 1,500-square-foot house was packed to the roof with aunts, uncles, cousins, grandparents, and as many church members as we could fit. The total count that day was forty-five living, breathing bodies in our brand-new home!

All of the women were eager to be of service, and there were as many women in the kitchen as there had been kernels of corn at the first Thanksgiving feast! I had a plan that I was not able to implement because of so many great "helpers." One of our beloved aunts, who had just finished carving a 35-pound turkey, set the platter on the stove due to the not-so-surprising fact that there was no counter space left. She did not realize that the burner was on, waiting for the gravy to be made, and the antique platter boasting the magnificent tom turkey exploded across the countertop. Everything that had a cover on it was salvageable, but the dressing (or the "stuffing, y'all" as his side called it) was filled with indefinable shards of glass. So, to start the meal, we had no turkey and no dressing...excuse me...I really did mean to say stuffing!

The crowd was growing anxious, and I knew that we had to eat quickly or the southerners and northerners would soon be re-enacting Gettysburg! I just had one last dish to take out of the oven, and it was my concession to pleasing the Southern in-laws: sweet potato soufflé complete with brown sugar, pecans, and a meringue topping! As I opened my very tired oven and reached in for the mountainous dish filled with sticky, delightful sweet potato delicacy, someone bumped into me, and I dropped the dish all over the kitchen floor. My kitchen had become an orange ice skating rink with sweet potatoes from one side to the other! Now, before we could eat, we had to hose down the kitchen! Everyone from both sides of the Mason-Dixon line was doing an admirable job controlling their horror, and no one was expressing the shared notion that this year they had accepted the wrong Thanksgiving invitation!

Just when I thought that it couldn't get any worse, our four-year-old son, Christopher, came downstairs looking for his daddy. Craig, of course, was in the kitchen trying to help me clean the floor, but more importantly, calm my frazzled, northern nerves.

Both of Christopher's grandfathers tried to help him the best that they could, but this little boy was adamant and demanded to see his daddy. We heard Christopher's cries from in the kitchen, and Craig went to see what was needed. As Craig bent down to look in Christopher's forlorn little eyes, he noticed that Christopher had just been to the bathroom and had not yet done up his little boy zipper.

"Here, buddy, let Daddy do up your zipper," Craig patiently said in spite of the tension of the day.

"But Daddy! We don't have time to do up my zipper. The potty has sprung a leak, and the upstairs bathroom floor looks like there is an ocean on it!" Craig and both of our fathers went bounding up the stairs just in time to see the water come splashing out of the bathroom and begin to soak our two-month-old carpet! Where was the Mayflower when you needed it?

At that very moment, the North and the South joined in one great guffaw, and we have spent every holiday together ever since sharing collard greens and mincemeat pie...squash and sweet potatoes...and we have all long since forgotten who calls it stuffing and who calls it dressing!

The dinner that year was not served in the dining room, but there were Mayflower descendants on the piano bench, the floor, and the front porch. Every single stair step had a child on it, some northern and some southern, but all enjoying a feast only equaled by that of the Pilgrims and the Indians. We all had much to be thankful for...even if there was no turkey...the kitchen floor oozed of sugar as it was walked upon...and we had some very wet upstairs carpeting!

***Presence and Provision***

The more I grow in Christ and become conformed to His image, and the longer I walk through life holding hands with Him, the more I realize that the dining room of my home cannot be equated with the dining room of my heart. The dining room of my home is used for times of celebration and holiday festivity; the dining room of my heart is utilized during the wilderness experiences of my life. The dining room of my heart is where Jesus and I sit down alone together and dine. It is where His presence is the sweetest and His abundance the most life-changing! The dining room of my heart is where my joy truly does not depend upon my circumstances or upon what I see with my natural eyes. This dining room-set aside for His presence and His provision - is the place of miracles in my destitute world!

### ***The Shape and Substance of the Wilderness***

Then Jesus was led up by the Spirit into the wilderness to be tempted by the devil. – **MATTHEW 4:1**

The Spirit - with a capital "S" - led Jesus into the wilderness. This scenario comes directly following the moment when Jesus was baptized in the Jordan River by John the Baptist. (See Matthew 3:13-17.) The wilderness experience comes immediately following the obedience of Jesus in baptism, the supernatural anointing by the Dove from on high, and hearing the voice of God speak His pleasure over His only Son's life! Matthew 3:16 records the fact that the Holy Spirit descended as a dove and lit on the shoulder of Jesus. Then this same Spirit - the Spirit who had anointed and confirmed the blessing of God the Father on Jesus the Son - led Jesus into the wilderness! Try to put that into your theology! Let me say it one more time so you understand the divine intent: The Spirit - with a capital "S" - led Jesus into the wilderness!

The Spirit led Jesus into the wilderness to be tempted by the devil. The word "tempted" literally means to put to the test to see what good or evil, strengths or weaknesses exist in a person. The wilderness experience of your life is a test to which you have been led by the Holy Spirit. This test is for a purpose: It is to see what good things are in your heart as well as what bad things have taken residence in your heart. It is to see where your weaknesses lie as well as where your strengths lie. The Spirit led Jesus into the wilderness not to see if He was ready but to show Him that He was ready!

Do you think that you are any different from Jesus? Jesus needed a wilderness experience to show Him that He was ready...do you think that you don't need a wilderness experience? The purpose of the wilderness is to show you once and for all that the power of Christ resides in you in strength and is ready to go to battle on your behalf.

The wilderness to which Jesus was led by the Holy Spirit was not like any wilderness remaining to be pioneered in the world today. But it was filled to repletion with wild animals and Jesus encountered scorpions...lions...and snakes! He might have come face to face with a growling, savage wolf. These animals were hungry - just days away from starvation. I do not even like domesticated dogs when I go on a walk through my very safe neighborhood! The wilderness that Jesus faced had fangs and growling stomachs. The landscape was jagged with uneven, warped cliffs and was both rocky and treacherous. It lay beside the Dead Sea, which is the lowest spot on earth. The wilderness to which Jesus had been led by the Spirit was filled to capacity with two commodities: intense heat and emptiness. There was no vegetation in this wilderness - only stones, dust, and sandstorms that would blow up at a moment's notice. Does this wilderness sound like any through which you have passed?

Possibly a divorce that you have recently endured could be described as the lowest spot on the face on of the earth. Maybe it was the death of a child that caused you to crash headfirst from the warped, jagged cliffs of grief. Financial ruin disguises itself as a wild animal that hunts and taunts and growls, and a broken heart is the scorching wind that blows through your life and decimates all vegetation.

I do not believe that Jesus brings divorce, financial ruin, or sickness into our lives. These tragedies are the jagged landscape that frame our wilderness, but they do not come from God. We serve a

Father who only brings good and perfect gifts. Our loving Father does not punish His children with circumstances gone awry. However, our Father, whose very nature is love, allows us to walk through the issues of life that seem to be, from our very limited human perspective, the stuff of which a wilderness is made.

Usually in the wilderness of life...like Jesus...you are all alone...painfully alone. When the wild animals begin to howl in the midnight hours, you are alone. When the hunger pains start to scream and there is no provision for sustenance, you are alone. When the wind blows around you and the sand fills your nostrils, you are alone.

***The Table***

Silently...quietly...into your wilderness walks the One who has been there before. The Man like no other, who settled His divinity in the wilderness two thousand years earlier, comes beside You, and instantly...miraculously...you are no longer alone. As you look into His eyes and become more aware of His presence than you are of the wilderness, you realize that Jesus has made provision for you in this experience. You look beyond the Man before you and see that in this intense heat, in the face of ferocious beasts and snarling animals, He has provided a table for you. Soon you are no longer aware of the dangerous topography of the land, but you are mesmerized by the banquet table, laden with gifts and treasures in the middle of it all.

***The Covering of His Presence***

> He who dwells in the shelter of the Most High will abide in the shadow of the Almighty. I will say to the LORD, "My refuge and my fortress, my God, in whom I trust!" For it is He who delivers

you from the snare of the trapper and from the deadly pestilence. He will cover you with His pinions, and under His wings you may seek refuge; His faithfulness is a shield and bulwark." – **PSALM 91:1-4**

As you stand unprotected from raging sandstorms, intense heat during the day, and extreme cold at night, Jesus covers you in the wilderness of your life. He surrounds you with all that He is and protects you under the refuge of His wings. The windstorms are no longer a hazard to your ability to breathe, nor do the wild animals pose a bodily threat because you have been covered.

The blessings of His covering are, first of all, that He will deliver you from the snare of the trapper and from the deadly pestilence. No longer is your life at risk in this wilderness because He will not allow the pestilence nor the snare to touch you...He has delivered you! Jesus has given you refuge from the storm under His covering. The refuge that He has provided is well able to withstand the force of category 5 hurricane winds, a blizzard of gargantuan proportions, or an earthquake that threatens to shake your world. His refuge is an impenetrable fortress in which you can seek refuge all the days of your life. The faithfulness of God will be a shield to you during the times of testing and temptations. His faithfulness, which is new every morning, will fight off the darts of the enemy and will shield you from the fire of the desert. It is the assurance that He will never change in the face of calamity, storms, famine, and the abundance of His provision in a dry and thirsty land. His faithfulness is sure-footed companionship on rocky and rugged terrain.

You will not be afraid of the terror by night, or of the arrow that flies by day; of the pestilence that stalks in the darkness, or of the destruction that lays waste at noon. – **PSALM 91:5-6**

When Jesus covers you with the comfort of His presence, no longer will fear be your constant tormentor. Nothing – not weapons, pestilence, or destruction – has the ability to cause your adrenaline to increase, your blood pressure to rise, or your mouth to go dry. These temporary, circumstantial conditions will not cause fear because you will be covered with the comfort of His presence.

> A thousand may fall at your side and ten thousand at your right hand, but it shall not approach you. – **PSALM 91:7**

His covering will protect you from your enemies no matter their names or their numbers. God is not intimidated by the forces of mass destruction that Satan configures, and neither should you be afraid! If cancer is the enemy...or rebellious children...or financial ruin...or the loneliness of a call to singleness...God has covered you and will protect you from the onslaught no matter how profound! Not only will these enemies have no power over your life, but also the Word says that God will not even allow them to approach you!

It is the assurance that He will never change in the face of calamity, storms and famine that becomes baundant provision in a dry and thirsty land.

> You will only look on with your eyes and see the recompense of the wicked. – **PSALM 91:8**

You will look and see the ravaging results of the destruction in the lives of those around you, but it will not even come near to your dwelling place. You will see it with your eyes, but you will not be touched by it. You will see things happen to others that will not touch you because you have been covered. All of this occurs in the dining room of your heart.

For you have made the LORD, my refuge, even the Most High, your dwelling place. – **PSALM 91:9**

There is a prerequisite to the blessing of His covering you in your wilderness places, and that is that you must make Him your dwelling place. As you travel through life and the Spirit leads you into a time of wilderness, do not deny yourself His protection and His shelter. You can choose His providential covering when you stay in the Word of God! If you have hidden the Word of God in your heart and have consistently spent time learning of Him through the written Word, then you will have the protection of His covering.

The importance of commitment to a body of believers is one of the most powerful choices that a believer can make. If you long for His protection and for His covering through all seasons of your life, then go to church! Stay in church! You will never find a perfect church with a perfect pastor, a perfect worship leader, and a perfect children's program. Seek God's heart, hear His voice concerning a body of believers, and then hunker in. Do not...let me repeat...do not...under any conditions leave that church due to disappointment or offense. You should only leave a local church for these three reasons: (1) You are making a geographical move; (2) the pastor has moved into heresy or sin; or (3) you have clearly heard God's voice moving you on in faith, not through disappointments, offenses, or pride. Once you have heard God's voice concerning your commitment to a body of believers, it is of vital importance that you fellowship with the family at that church. Please do not hold yourself aloof or at an arm's length or sit in the back row and run out as soon as service ends. Building relationships, serving at the church, and taking advantage of all that church has to offer will bring both vitality and stability to your walk with God. It is the local church that will be your covering as you walk through the wilderness of life.

The most practical way that I know to make God your dwelling place is to worship passionately! During the early years of our marriage, I held myself in check during worship services at our church. After all, my husband was the pastor, and I did not want to be guilty of drawing undue attention to myself. I would sing quietly, raise my hands half-heartedly, and rarely clap. Now, in my heart, I was dancing just as David did, but I dare not let myself become a spectacle to our congregation! It was during a time of deep, emotional trauma that the Holy Spirit led me to a new level of worship. I was so desperate for His presence that what the church thought about my passionate worship no longer mattered. I was able to allow the tears to flow, my hands to be raised high in the air, and to lift my voice in song! When you allow yourself to worship with reckless abandon, you are making Him your dwelling place, and you have His promise that He will cover you during all the storms of your life!

Be still, and know that I am God. **– PSALM 46:10, NKJV**

Oftentimes in the wilderness experiences of life, you just have to cease striving and know that He is control and well able to complete that which He has promised. When you have hidden the Word in your heart, have been faithfully committed to a body of believers, have entered a new level of worship in your life, and are still in the middle of the wilderness...then just be still and know that He is your God. This is the exact moment in your walk with Christ that you have made Him your dwelling place, and you are abiding in the shadow of the Most High. He will be your protective covering through all of the deserts and valleys of life. You have finally come to the point where you are more at home in His presence than you are anywhere on earth. You have made Him your dwelling place!

What a grand and safe place to live! Where do you really live? Do you live in your circumstances, or do you live in His presence?

### *The Shadow of His Covering*

> Be gracious to me, O God, be gracious to me, for my soul takes refuge in You; and in the shadow of Your wings I will take refuge until destruction passes by. I will cry to God Most High, to God who accomplishes all things for me. – **PSALM 57:1-2**

If you still can not comprehend the sweet mystery of dwelling in His presence, then pray the prayer of Psalm 57:1-2 one thousand times a day! After my sons left for college and I was teetering on the edge of depression, I would open my Bible to Psalm 57 every morning. I prayed with every ounce of faith that I could muster, "Jesus, be gracious to me today because I am an emotional mess! Lord, I long for Your presence to be more real to me than the reality of my circumstances. I do not take refuge in my circumstances, but I am hiding myself in YOU and all that YOU are! Lord, wrap Your strong arms around me until I get through this emotional quicksand. God, Your ways are higher than my ways, and You are well able to accomplish great and mighty things on my behalf! I believe it with my whole heart!"

God was faithful during those days of emotional desperation. I found the shadow of His wings to be a place of protection from the storm that I was enduring. Dwelling in Him and staying in the shadow of His presence was a cool spot away from the intense heat of the desert sun. He was covering me once again.

> When I remember You on my bed, I meditate on You in the night watches, for You have been my help, and in the shadow of Your wings I sing for joy. – **PSALM 63:6-7**

These verses from the beloved Book of Psalms introduce us to yet one more benefit of His abundant covering, and that is the knowledge that when we are abiding in the shadow of His wings (which is His covering), we are able to sing for joy! If we are not dwelling under the shadow of His wings, we will never experience the ability to sing in the night. When we are experiencing His protection and His covering, we are intimately aware of His presence. It is when we are covered by His presence that we experience a new ability to praise and worship Him!

I have found worship to be the sweetest when I am struggling through a wilderness experience in my life. When I am in the desert of life, my emotions are roaring like a vicious windstorm, and I choose to stay under the protective blanket of His covering, it is then that I realize what praise and worship are really all about. Anyone can praise Him in the times of abundance and safety, but if you can praise Him while the wind is howling, the landscape is treacherous, and you are facing the fangs of the enemy - then you know what a song of joy was intended to be! You sing because you are covered by His presence! You sing because there is only one strategy for victory, and that is under His covering! You sing because He is enough...He is more than enough! His covering has become your favorite blanket, and you will never go through the wilderness without it again!

***It's Raining Bread!***

> The whole congregation of the sons of Israel grumbled against Moses and Aaron in the wilderness. The sons of Israel said to them, "Would that we had died by the LORD'S hand in the land of Egypt, when we sat by the pots of meat, when we ate bread to the full; for you have brought us out into this

> wilderness to kill this whole assembly with hunger." Then the LORD said to Moses, "Behold, I will rain bread from heaven for you; and the people shall go out and gather a day's portion every day, that I may test them, whether or not they will walk in My instruction. On the sixth day, when they prepare what they bring in, it will be twice as much as they gather daily." So Moses and Aaron said to all the sons of Israel, "At evening you will know that the LORD has brought you out of the land of Egypt; and in the morning you will see the glory of the LORD, for He hears your grumblings against the LORD, and what are we that you grumble against us?"– **EXODUS 16:2-7**

This account from Exodus tells the story of God's children, the Israelites, who were the apple of His eye. They were His chosen people, and He had delivered them out of Egypt from the hand of Pharaoh, who was using the Israelites as his slaves. God had supernaturally saved His children, and now they were complaining! The children of Israel were remembering that although they were slaves in Egypt, at least they were well fed! Not only were the Israelites complaining about the lack of food, but they were also whining about the ability of Moses and Aaron to lead them. God loved them in spite of their whining, complaining, and self-centered attitudes, and He said, "I will send bread from heaven!" God promised Moses and Aaron that He was going to bless these whining wimps in spite of their bad attitudes. God knew that the wilderness was not an easy place to be, and He chose to provide in abundance for His children even when they were complaining.

I love this provision in the wilderness! What fun! It's raining bread! Regardless of my attitude - and oh! How I want a good attitude that will bring glory to Him! - it's raining bread! Next time you are in the wilderness - even if you are whining, complaining, and questioning the sovereignty of God - look up! It's raining bread for your benefit and for your provision! It's raining bread for His glory!

> Jesus said to them, "Truly, truly, I say to you, it is not Moses who has given you the bread out of heaven, but it is My Father who gives you the true bread out of heaven. For the bread of God is that which comes down out of heaven and gives life to the world." Then they said to Him, "Lord, always give us this bread." Jesus said to them, 'I am the bread of life; he who comes to Me will not hunger, and he who believes in Me will never thirst." – **JOHN 6:32-35**

I believe that every single event in the Old Testament pointed toward the coming of Jesus as Messiah of the world. When God provided manna in the wilderness and the children of God experienced the miracle of bread raining down from heaven, even this event was a foreshadowing of the provision that God would give through His Son, Jesus Christ. These verses in John reiterate the fact that Jesus is our Bread of Life. He is our provision from God the Father in every wilderness that we walk through on earth. When God sent provision to the Israelites in the desert, that manna that He sent was representative of Jesus Christ Himself! It was the presence of Jesus in the form of manna that was providing for them when they were complaining. It was the presence of Jesus that was sustaining them although they chose to whine, murmur, and complain. It was the Bread of Life in the wilderness that proved the miraculous presence of God was with them!

> He humbled you and let you be hungry, and fed you with manna which you did not know, nor did your fathers know, that

> He might make you understand that man does not live by bread alone, but man lives by everything that proceeds out of the mouth of the LORD....In the wilderness He fed you manna which your fathers did not know, that He might humble you and that He might test you, to do good for you in the end. Otherwise, you may say in your heart, "My power and the strength of my hand made me this wealth."
> **– DEUTERONOMY 8: 3, 16-17**

God dealt graciously with His children in the wilderness, and He deals graciously with you as well. In the wilderness, God provided His presence, His abundance, His Word, and His strength, which were all manifested through the raining down of bread. God knew that it was necessary for this provision to be a daily provision. He rained down just enough of the bread of His presence to get His children through one day at a time.

If indeed it is true that man does not live by bread alone but by every Word that proceeds out of the mouth of God, what was the manna? Was it mere bread? Was it a representation of His presence? Was it a representation of the Word of God? Manna, in the wilderness of our lives, represents the Word of God. It represents the strength that the Word of God gives and the power to overcome, which is only attained through the daily reading of the Word of God. We need His Word every single day of our lives - especially when we are going through the wilderness! His desire is to provide for you regardless of the condition of your heart. In the dining room of your heart, which is the wilderness experience, first He covers you under the shadow of His wings, and then He provides His presence for you. He provides food for sustenance and the Word for strength. Look up! It's raining bread!

> The house of Israel named it manna, and it was like coriander seed, white, and its taste was like wafers with honey.
> – **EXODUS 16:31**

Coriander seed was known in biblical times for its ability to heal and was used chiefly for medicinal purposes. God's Word will heal you in every wilderness experience in your life. If you stay in the Word of God every single day, your attitudes will be healed! God's Word has healing power in our lives, and its power is in direct proportion to the dosage that we choose to ingest! Devour the Word of God every day in large amounts and the healing that takes place in your heart will be miraculous!

This manna, which was the bread that was rained down from heaven, had the distinct taste of honey. The taste of manna was a prophetic taste of what was to come for the children of Israel, for they were about to enter a land that was flowing with milk and honey! The Word of God, which was represented by the manna from heaven, has the ability to sweeten the wilderness experience of your life. If you stay in the Word and make it your main diet during this time in the desert, you will have no remembrance of the rocky cliffs or the scorpions that threatened to poison you; you will only remember the sweetness of His presence that sustained you every day! The psalmist said it this way: "How sweet are Your words to my taste! Yes, sweeter than honey to my mouth!" (Ps. 119:103).

### *Soaring Over the Wilderness*

> And the LORD spoke to Moses, saying, "I have heard the grumblings of the sons of Israel; speak to them, saying, 'At twilight you shall eat meat, and in the morning you shall be filled with bread; and you shall know that I am the LORD your God.'" So it came about at evening that the quails came up and

> covered the camp, and in the morning there was a layer of dew around the camp. – **EXODUS 16:11-13**

Quail was the third provision that God gave to the children of Israel while they were in the wilderness. God chose to feed His children with this type of flying bird not by chance or coincidence. God, who does nothing out of happenstance, chose quail for a very particular reason. Quail have strong flying muscles and are able to fly very quickly for short distances. However, quail know what to do when they reach the end of their own strength. Quail, at the end of their avian strength, stretch out their wings and allow the wind to bear them along. On their own, quail would only be able to fly short distances, but when they allow the wind to carry them, they are able to migrate long distances.

God chose quail as a picture for all of us who feel trapped in the wilderness of life and as a reminder that when we try to travel through life on our own strength, we never make the progress that is possible until we allow the wind of the Holy Spirit to carry us. Our own strength is adequate only for short distances, but His Spirit will carry us to destinations of which we never dreamed! Don't do life on your own strength...catch the wind of the Spirit!

***The Ordinary Becomes Extraordinary***

> Then the LORD said to Moses, "Pass before the people and take with you some of the elders of Israel; and take in your hand your staff with which you struck the Nile, and go. Behold, I will stand before you there on the rock at Horeb; and you shall strike the rock, and water will come out of it, that the people may drink." And Moses did so in the sight of the elders of Israel.
> – **EXODUS 17:5-6**

God will not only provide water in the dry, desert places of your life, but He will also bring it through miraculous means! If God provided fresh, spring water in the wilderness for the Israelites who were a bunch of whining, complaining, ungrateful wimps...just think what He will do for us as we go through our wilderness with praise! God will give you times of cool refreshment as you travel through the lowest places in your life. God will send people who will pray for you, and it will be like a glass of clear, sparkling water on a hot, summer day! A verse will miraculously catch your attention during your daily Bible reading, and it will feel as if you are running through a mountain stream! God will send a check in the mail...a loaf of home-baked bread...or a bouquet of fresh gardenias, and that will be like a well-watered garden on a rocky cliff of life!

> He split the rocks in the wilderness and gave them abundant drink like the ocean depths. He brought forth streams also from the rock and caused waters to run down like rivers.
> – **PSALM 78:15-16**

Water always causes the growth of new life! When God sends amazing water like ocean depths into your wilderness, you will be satisfied knowing that there is nothing too difficult for your God in the dead places of the desert. If He can break open a rock and give abundant drink, then He is well able to satisfy and cause new life to grow and water your dead places!

> For I do not want you to be unaware, brethren, that our fathers were all under the cloud and all passed through the sea; and all were baptized into Moses in the cloud and in the sea; and all ate the same spiritual food; and all drank the same spiritual drink, for they were drinking from a spiritual rock which followed them; and the rock was Christ. – **1 CORINTHIANS 10:1-4**

The water of which you drink deeply in the wilderness is not natural water made from molecules of hydrogen and oxygen. That which satisfies in the wilderness is not bottled, carbonated, or imported. The spiritual drink that is yours in abundance during the desert times of your life's journey is from the Rock...with a capital "R"! Jesus, your Rock, will perform miracles on your behalf when you go to Him during the hardest times of your life. The newspaper will not comfort you, a self-help book will only bring temporary relief, and a counselor has no real power in your life other than to lead you to the Rock who is your strong tower in times of storm!

God always gives water and performs miracles that will bring glory to His name. Water, in the Bible, without exception denotes that a miracle is on its way! When the children of Israel were confronted by the water of the Red Sea, God came to their defense and parted the water for His children! When God's children were hemmed in by the wilderness on every side and were desperate for water, God struck the rock, and water came flowing out in supernatural abundance! When Jesus, the Son of God on earth, was invited to a wedding and the wine supply had been depleted, Jesus took water and turned it into wine! That is the nature of God...to take something ordinary and turn it into something extraordinary.

He did it for the Israelites...He did it at the wedding in Canaan...and He will do it for you as well!

***The Work of Fire***

> The LORD was going before them in a pillar of cloud by day to lead them on the way, and in a pillar of fire by night to give them light, that they might travel by day and by night. He did not take away the pillar of cloud by day, nor the pillar of fire by night, from before the people. – **EXODUS 13:21-22**

In order to be delivered from the wilderness, you have to know the way out. You must discover the paths or routes that have been provided for your deliverance. It is necessary to read God's roadmaps...not your roadmaps. You have to hear His voice and then follow His leading. God will speak to you through the Word, but you must choose to follow His will and His ways, which are always higher than our ways. Your ways will merely become a maze of confusion in which you will become eternally trapped. His ways are clear and smooth...but higher than your ways. God provides the pillar of fire to give you light so that you can find the way out of this wilderness filled with threatening situations.

The light that God gives to His children in the wilderness is a pillar of fire. This fire that God sends into the darkest hour of your life will burn up anything that does not belong in your life. God will use His fire to burn the weeds, the underbrush, and the thorns. He will clean up your grumblings, your bad attitudes, and your impatience. These things might be what got you into the wilderness in the first place! God will incinerate all of the trash in your life that is keeping you in the wilderness. For most of us, just like the Israelites, what is necessary to be decimated by fire is our rotten, stinking attitudes. It is our bent to complain rather than to praise that should be ravaged by fire, or our need to question God rather than to trust Him. Many times, the weeds in my life that need burning are the feelings that my way is the best and I just really don't need to consult God on this issue. Many times in my life, a bad habit or sin has kept me in the wilderness, but God has always provided the fire to burn it up! The fire of God will always purify that which is keeping us from His best and will direct us in the way of deliverance.

The sad truth of the matter is that many Christians never make it out of the wilderness. Oh, they are covered under the shadow of His wing...they will be well fed with the bread that has rained down from heaven...they will even experience the power of the Holy Spirit that bears us up when we are weary...some will see miracles take place as He pours water into their life situations. But a sad number of Christians will not allow the fire of God to do its work in their lives, and so the wilderness becomes their home. They are wandering around in a maze that has been fashioned by their own willful decisions to do life in their own strength and according to their own roadmap.

> "It will come about in all the land," declares the LORD, "that two parts in it will be cut off and perish; but the third will be left in it. And I will bring the third part through the fire, refine them as silver is refined, and test them as gold is tested. They will call on My name, and I will answer them. I will say, 'They are My people,' and they will say, 'The LORD is my God.'"
> **– ZECHARIAH 13:8-9**

If you will allow the fire to burn out the dross of your life, you will be refined to exactly the sheen and substance of silver. If you will allow the fire of God to consume the attitudes, habits, and sins that have kept you in the maze, you will be in a position where you will be able to hear the voice of God. If you will allow the fire of His presence to guide you and then go His way and not your own, you will be delivered from the wilderness!

### *You Have What It Takes!*

You will find yourself in the expansive dining room at your Father's home. Feasting on manna with its sweetness and its ability to heal, you will be experiencing miracles in life that only the Rock can call forth! In your Dad's dining room, you will be covered with His presence, and you will laugh for sheer joy as you soar with the wind of the Holy Spirit! You will never again be the same as you enter the abundant dining room that your Father has provided, because you will have been changed in the wilderness of life. The wilderness is a test...not to see if you are ready to serve your Father, but to show you that you are ready! You have what it takes to make a difference this side of heaven and to live a life filled with His abundance! You have what it takes to soar high above the thunderclouds and to sing in the night!

> Egypt was glad when they departed, for the dread of them had fallen upon them. He spread a cloud for a covering, and fire to illumine by night. They asked, and He brought quail, and satisfied them with the bread of heaven. He opened the rock and water flowed out; it ran in the dry places like a river. For He remembered His holy word with Abraham His servant; and He brought forth His people with joy, His chosen ones with a joyful shout. He gave them also the lands of the nations, that they might take possession of the fruit of the peoples' labor, so that they might keep His statutes and observe His laws. Praise the LORD! – **PSALM 105: 38-45**

The purpose of the wilderness is to prove to you that you have the capacity to sing for joy in all of life's circumstances! When you sing for joy in the face of trauma, trial, and tragedy, you will take possession of all of the nations. Your neighborhood will turn to God, your unsaved family will come into the Kingdom, and everyone that you touch will obey your powerful and mighty God! The wilderness was not about you, but it was about the people's lives that you would touch because of the shout that resounded through all of the valleys of your life!

### *Dining in His Presence*

Then the devil left Him; and behold, angels came and began to minister to Him. – **MATTHEW 4:11**

As you leave your wilderness, you will experience the presence of ministering angels who quietly and carefully tend. These are angels who bring no divine message but who hover with the comfort of His presence.

You only thought that you were alone in the darkness and on the parched land. You only thought that you were all by yourself when the wild animals howled long into the lonely nights. You only imagined that no one was with you when the wind was roaring and the hunger pains were screaming. But when you turn and look back at the wilderness, you will finally realize that you have never been alone. His presence has been with you on every sharp rock, in every barren place, and during each sleepless night. You will know for certain as you look back that you found joy in the wilderness because His presence was your guide. He has been sitting at the table in your wilderness from the moment that you entered this loathsome place and was patiently waiting for your company. He has filled a table ladened with abundant provisions. The wilderness of your life has become the dining room filled with His presence and His abundance! This is the truth of the dining room of your heart. Only a Christian can walk through cancer with joy! Only a believer who is filled with love for the Savior can say, "My job is not my source! God is my source!" Only someone who has made Christ the strong tower of her life can proclaim, "I might have a broken heart, but the Word of God says that God is near to the brokenhearted!" Only Christians can walk through the wilderness and experience miraculous transformation in the dining room of His presence!

*Chapter Seven*

# THE FAMILY ROOM

When was the last time that you shouted? You know...the kind of yell that can't be suppressed and releases all of the pent-up excitement that has been stored in your heart? It might have been a primal Indian whoop...a cheerleader's victory chant...or a childlike shout of glee on Christmas morning. Once in a while, you have to shout and just let loose!

When was the last time that you literally danced for joy? My grandmother called it "doing the jig!" I can still see her doing the jig in her kitchen...across the green linoleum floor with her little Irish heels kicking high in the air. Athletes call this type of response "the victory dance," and they love doing it in the end zone! How long has it been since you danced with your husband across the living room to the romantic rhapsody known as "our song"?

How about a belly laugh? The kind of laughter that comes from deep, down inside and that you could not hold back if you tried. I love the laughter of babies with their innocent little giggles that expand into chortles and finally into belly-shaking glee! I am not referring to a precious little "tee-hee" that is expressed in a simper that can be hidden behind your linen handkerchief. When was the last time you were laughing so hard that the tears were streaming down your cheeks...your sides were splitting...you could no longer breathe...and you just may have been leaking from some improper places!

Life is short, and we need to sing...to dance...to shout...to celebrate! When living life with a capital "L," there is no time to be wasted in mopey mornings and days of depressive endings. It is time to clean up the family room of your heart and throw a party! Let's turn up the music and send out invitations!

***Zoe Life!***

One day when I was in college, I was sent to the office of one of the university deans for some academic business. I arrived in the outer area of his suite of offices and informed the secretary why I had come. She told me that while the dean was not in, I could go sit in his office and wait for him. As she ushered me into a room that was filled with scholarly journals and theological treatises, I was captured by the picture that hung over the desk of this man of international importance. In the center of the wall, between doctoral and master's degrees from prestigious institutions, was a picture of Jesus with his mouth open wide and sheer glee written all over His lovely face. Jesus was experiencing a moment of earthly joy, and He felt the freedom to express His pleasure in laughter! The picture was so real that I could almost hear the cadence of the explosive sound of the guffaw that had come from the heart of my Savior! I wonder if this was the picture of Jesus that may have been painted following the words, "I have come that they may have life, and that they may have it more abundantly" (John 10:10, NKJV).

In these verses from John chapter 10, Jesus was referring to *zoe*, which is one of three Greek words for life. *Zoe* life is not the living and breathing kind of life that is found in biological matter. This *zoe* life has nothing to do with your heart, lungs, or bodily functions. When the Bible refers to the kind of life that has a definite beginning and ending, the word used is *bios*. *Bios* life is extensive life or the period or duration of your life. *Bios* life could be described as the dash on your tombstone. Your *psuche* life refers to your mind or intellect. *Psuche* life is what you learn from the day you are born until the day that you die. It is the intellectual responses of your brain to the world around you and to the people that you meet. Whereas *bios* life is extensive, *zoe* life is intensive. *Zoe* life is how well you live or the vitality with which you live your life. The only possible similarity between *zoe* life and *bios* life is adrenaline. This is the only place where these two very different types of life meet for a moment. Adrenaline is a biological secretion from the adrenal glands that stimulates the heart. Your adrenaline starts pumping as a response to excitement. When you were young, your heart would start beating rapidly and your breathing would increase as you were filled with the anticipation and excitement of the first day of school...or a visit from your grandparents. If you are living a *zoe* life, it means that you are living life with great gusto and are giving your adrenal glands a thorough workout! *Zoe* life means that you live life with appetite and pleasure!

Before you picture *zoe* life as some hedonistic free-for-all, let me assure you that the source of *zoe* life is God! The only origin of *zoe* life is from the heart of God who gives us richly all things to enjoy! The source of *bios* life is the genetic structure inherited from your parents; the source of *psuche* life is the books that you have read, the classes in which you have enrolled, and the men and women under whose tutelage you have acquired knowledge. *Zoe* life is the noblest form of life, and therefore it is all of the highest and best that the saints possess in God. *Zoe* is contained in joy, peace, righteousness, and purity.

When Jesus spoke the words in John 10:10, He did not say, "I have come that My sheep might have *bios* life and *bios* life in abundance." Nor did He exclaim, "I have come that My sheep might have *psuche* life and have *psuche* life in abundance." When Jesus came, He announced with great enthusiasm, "I have come that My sheep might have *zoe* life and might have *zoe* life in abundance!"

The life that Jesus brings is not a pious, boring existence that causes Christians to have sour expressions on their face and frown at the slightest hint of fun. Jesus was many things, but religious was not one of them. He did not have a religious bone in His precious body! He was not about religion but about relationship, and He brought *zoe* life to this world of ours!

An exuberant personality is not necessarily the hallmark of a life lived with the *zoe* touch of God. *Zoe* life is not the bent of some personality types to be the life of every party. The potential to live a *zoe* life exists in the heart of every man, woman, and child regardless of personality, upbringing, or scars. This room in your heart that I have dubbed the family room is not decorated by one's personality or by one's past; rather it is decorated by your relationship with the Giver of *zoe* life: Jesus Christ Himself!

I loved the chaplain at Oral Roberts University (ORU) during the days that I was a student and later when I worked at the university as the women's chaplain. "Brother Bob," as he was affectionately called by the students, left a lifetime impression upon my heart because he had a way of expressing the joy found in the Word of God that was heart stirring yet so simple. He continually told the students, "We have something to be so happy about that nothing can ever really be sad again."

If your happiness is based upon your circumstances, you will be waiting a long time to plan a party in the family room of your heart. However, if your happiness is based upon a relationship with the One who died for you, then your life has the potential to be filled with the *zoe* life of God! I have a feeling that when we get to heaven and gaze back upon our earthly life, we will realize that we had so much more to be glad about than we ever realized! I have a feeling that when we get to heaven and turn our eyes back to this earthly kingdom, we will realize that we could have...and should have...lived a *zoe* life! I suspect that when we get to heaven and reminisce about the life that we lived while on earth, we will realize that most things that stole our joy were deceptive tools of the enemy used to cripple us and rob us of the potential to live a *zoe* life!

Let's do life God's way and not live our lives crippled by circumstances or framed by our personalities. Our lives must be lived with great enthusiasm and pleasure knowing that all good and perfect gifts are from above. Let's live a *zoe* life!

### *Plan to Live a Zoe Life*

If your heart's desire is to live the *zoe* life that Jesus promised, the first step is to PLAN! PLAN to be a *zoe* person every day of your life. When you wake up in the morning, ask yourself the question, "What can I do today to live a *zoe* life?" I have purposed in my heart that I will PLAN to live a *zoe* life. The best parties I have ever attended were parties that were well planned, and conversely, some parties never take place because people do not plan them. Will you plan a *zoe* life party? Will you choose to meet all of life's circumstances with joy, peace, righteousness, and purity? That is life at its finest and is the way that God intended for His children to live out their days on earth!

"This is the day which the LORD has made; let us rejoice and be glad in it" (Ps.118:24) If indeed you believe that the verse is true, then you will PLAN to rejoice and be glad every day that God gives to you here on earth. It is an act of your will and a conscious choice you will make every single day. When you lay your head on the pillow at night, the last words thought before drifting off to sleep should be, "I can't wait for tomorrow! I PLAN to rejoice and be glad tomorrow! I PLAN to allow the *zoe* life of Christ to exude from every cell of my body! I will enter His gates with thanksgiving in my heart, I will enter His courts with praise!" (See Psalm 100:4.)

Will you? Will you plan to be a person of great thanksgiving and praise? Will you partake of Thanksgiving dinner every day of your life...or just one day a year? Will you purpose in your heart to praise Him when your children all have the chicken pox at once, when you are so lonely that you could cry, or when your checkbook only knows one color: red! Will you PLAN a praise party? Or will you PLAN a pity party? You must be aware that it is up to you. Jesus has placed within your heart the potential to live your life with zoe gusto.

One of my favorite people in the whole world is a young woman who has a great job, is involved at church, and loves to knit. She finds supreme delight and purpose in going on missions trips to help needy children in third world countries and in spending time with her nieces and nephews. Mary has chosen to live a *zoe* life even though her life has not lived up to her expectations. Mary was married to the man of her dreams and was deeply in love with him. She thought the feelings were mutual, until one day he came home and said, "I have found another woman." When Mary's world came crashing down around her, she made two willful decisions. She decided that she would absolutely not become a bitter person and that she would continue to be a woman of great praise and thanksgiving! Mary PLANNED to live a *zoe* life even though her life ripped apart at the seams. Mary knows that the secret of living a *zoe* life is found not in her circumstances but in her relationship with Jesus. *Zoe* overcomes disappointment and rules over tragedy.

All of life's trauma and unmet expectations must bow at the feet of Jesus, who is the Giver of *zoe* life!

> What shall I render to the LORD for all His benefits toward me? I shall lift up the cup of salvation and call upon the name of the LORD. I shall pay my vows to the LORD, oh may it be in the presence of His people. Precious in the sight of the LORD is the death of His godly ones. O LORD, surely I am Your servant, I am Your servant, the son of Your handmaid; You have loosed my bonds. To You I shall offer a sacrifice of thanksgiving, and call upon the name of the LORD. – **PSALM 116:12-17**

The psalmist asks a question that resounds through the ages. "What could I possibly give to the Lord or ever offer in response to His goodness toward me?" The answer is a simple response: God always requires a sacrifice. No longer does He require the blood of a lamb upon the altar because Jesus is the final Sacrifice of that kind. What God requires of us is a sacrifice of praise in response to His supreme goodness to us and to His blessing upon our lives. He requires that we live a lifestyle of thanksgiving and joy! He asks that we PLAN to live a *zoe* life! Many times, when you make this willful choice, it will be a sacrifice. It is not easy to dance a victory dance when the promotion went to someone less qualified than you. It is not easy to shout with enthusiasm when the doctor says, "It doesn't look good." It is not easy to sing a song of joy when your best friend is getting married and you are still suffering from the pain of a broken heart. God did not ask for an easy response...He asked for a sacrifice.

I hope that you will learn the lesson of verse 15 in the Scripture listed above: "Precious in the sight of the LORD is the death of His godly ones." We do not look at death the way that God views death.

We may think that something is painful while He thinks that it is precious. We may think that an event is tragedy, and He may see it as triumphant! We do not look at hard things the way that God looks at them. Every challenge in life is an opportunity to choose joy over pain!

This is the reason that you can PLAN to live a *zoe* life: It is because you are not the guest of honor; He is! If you think that your life is all about you, then get ready to decorate with black balloons and wilted flowers. Your life is not about you at all, but it is about living your life to honor Him...the One in whose presence is fullness of joy!

***Throw Out the Trash***

Cleanup is the very worst part of the party for me. The dishes may stay in my sink for days, and there is the remnant of decorations sometimes for months afterwards. In March I still have Christmas decorations lingering around...and in July, I have to take down the March Madness signs in order to display the red, white, and blue. As they say in the South, I can flat plan a party, but in order to clean the place up, I should probably hire a ten-woman crew!

Let me assure you, that there is a converse order of operations in planning a *zoe* life party. The cleanup happens not following the party, but actually, the cleanup happens well in advance of the opportunity to celebrate! There is some stuff in the family room of your heart that is hindering your ability to plan a *zoe* life party. There are some things that you need to go through, set by the roadside, and let the trash man come and haul away! Please don't have a yard sale with your trash. Please do not set your garbage out and then try to pawn it off on the neighborhood. Nobody wants your issues...they cost way too much, and they are in absolutely rotten condition!

> See to it that no one comes short of the grace of God; that no root of bitterness springing up causes trouble, and by it many be defiled. – **HEBREWS 12:15**

Many women that I know need to rid themselves of a jar of poison that is sitting under the sink of their hearts. This poison, disguised gracefully by a stiff upper lip, bears the name "bitterness." If you have any bitterness at all in your heart, your life will merely remain *bios* or, at the best, grow into an existence filled with *psuche*. Bitterness will annihilate any potential at all that you have of planning a *zoe* life party. Hanging on to your bitterness can be compared to drinking poison and thinking that the other person is going to die. Bitterness will only poison you and limit your ability to live life to the fullest with His peace, joy, righteousness, and purity.

Bitterness is holding on to anger and unforgiveness by allowing the unresolved issues to simmer, boil, and then grow until the poisonous concoction overtakes your entire life. Bitterness will cripple your ability to live a *zoe* life. You will be poisoned to the extent that you will barely be able to breathe, which will necessitate being placed on a heart and lung machine. That's not living...that is dying a slow, painful death. What is the antidote to this poison known as bitterness? What is the Ipecac that will diffuse the effects of this killing potion? The antidote is forgiveness. If you have allowed bitterness to wrap you in its death grip until you have become no more than a walking zombie, the prescription is to forgive!

> Be kind to one another, tender-hearted, forgiving each other, just as God in Christ also has forgiven you.– **EPHESIANS 4:32**

Another issue that is sure to put a damper on any attempt to throw a party full of *zoe* life is the distraction of gossip! If you have a problem with gossip, please do not crash my party! You are not on my invitation list, and the welcome mat will disappear faster than you can say, "Did you hear about...?" Furthermore, if you are a gossip, do not invite me to your party because I will not come!

> And just as they did not see fit to acknowledge God any longer, God gave them over to a depraved mind, to do those things which are not proper, being filled with all unrighteousness, wickedness, greed, evil; full of envy, murder, strife, deceit, malice; they are gossips, slanderers, haters of God...
> **– ROMANS 1:28-30**

How would you like the Bible to describe you in this way? If you are a gossip, you are also a slanderer and a hater of God! What is gossip? It is repeating a morsel of knowledge about another person. The morsel may be true or untrue – that is besides the fact. Gossip is emotional murder, and Christians should have no part in it! Do you need to clean gossip out of your life once and for all?

> He who goes about as a slanderer reveals secrets, therefore do not associate with a gossip. **– PROVERBS 20:19**

The Bible says not to even associate with a gossip! Not only is gossip a serious personal sin, but also being in the presence of a gossip will poison your soul as well. If you have a problem with repeating information concerning other people, make a decision right now that you will no longer talk about people. Do not talk about people! Refuse – from deep within your soul – to tarnish the reputation of another person made in the image of God. "Death and life are in the power of the tongue" (Prov. 18:21). You have the power to commit first-degree murder with the muscle that lies between your teeth. Many of us need to go on trial for premeditated murder because we have assassinated someone's reputation. If you have chosen to talk about your pastor in an unkind manner, you have committed murder against a spiritual leader. No wonder we struggle with living a *zoe* life! If you are a gossip or have a problem with bitterness, there are trash bags lining the walls of the family room of your heart, and you need to throw them out once and for all! The putrid smell that is emanating from the trash bags of bitterness and gossip could cause the paint on the walls to shrivel up and peel off. It's time to clean up your family room if you want to have a party!

### *Your "Hit List"*

> What was from the beginning, what we have heard, what we have seen with our eyes, what we have looked at and touched with our hands, concerning the Word of Life - and the life was manifested, and we have seen and testify and proclaim to you the eternal life which was with the Father and was manifested to us - what we have seen and heard we proclaim to you also, so that you too may have fellowship with us; and indeed our fellowship is with the Father, and with His Son Jesus Christ. These things we write, so that our joy may be made complete.
> **– 1 JOHN 1:1-4**

What we have experienced in our life in Christ is so outrageously wonderful that we absolutely have to share it! I am not able to keep it inside any longer, and therefore I must have a party and touch my world with His *zoe* life! Usually when you plan a party, it is in honor of someone else. When you plan a party, you should not be the guest of honor. It is improper etiquette to plan a baby shower when you are the one expecting. It is nothing short of obnoxious to send out invitations to a wedding shower for yourself.

The purpose of living this exciting, thrilling *zoe* life is not to bless yourself...but it is to bless others! The goal of living a *zoe* life is to touch the lives of everyone with whom you come in contact with the joy of His presence! There is great power in living a *zoe* life, and the power will impact your crabby boss, the lonely widow across the street, and that relative who turns every holiday celebration into World War III!

It is pure joy to touch others with His *zoe* life! Let me challenge you to make a "hit list" of the people in your world who need to be touched with the *zoe* life of Christ. Then, every time your path crosses theirs, you will be prepared with a word of encouragement, a smile, or a great nugget of conversation. You may even want to invite them to your home and share the joy of His presence with them in a heartfelt way. Buy every person on that list a gift, and look for an opportunity to give it to them! If you are indeed living life the *zoe* way, you will need to update this list about twice a year because you will be making a difference in these people's lives! You will need to add new names to your list because the names on your first list are now living their own *zoe* life! As you prayerfully make this list, your heart should be beating with purpose and literally pulsating with adrenaline as you realize that you have discovered the secret of how to touch your world with the joy of the Lord!

Many times when I have had a party in my home, it has been for the purpose of demonstrating a product so the guests can experience it firsthand. If you are a woman, living in the twenty-first century in the Western World, you have been invited to way too many of these product demonstration parties! What will they think of next? Makeup and perfume, cookware, toys, dresses, books, lingerie, illegal purses – I have been to them all! (Of course, I did not buy anything at the illegal purse party!) The intent behind a party at which the hostess demonstrates a product is that the guests can touch it, perhaps try it on, and maybe taste it! I have discovered that at the parties where a product is demonstrated, it is important for the hostess to know the product very well! That is why I could never sponsor a party for cookware – there is just no way that I could ever be an expert in how to cook! The party would flop, I would be embarrassed, and everyone would certainly go home with empty stomachs! If you intend to have a product demonstration party with your life, it would be wise to have read the Manual a time or two!

Our lives should be a party thrown in His honor and to demonstrate who He is and what He has done for us!

***Decorating Your Heart***

The family room of your heart should be no less than fabulous! There should be bright colors splashed liberally and brilliantly on every wall. This is the one room in the entire house that should take your breath away as you walk in the door. There should be pillows on the floor and on furniture – just waiting for a rambunctious pillow fight or to be a comfortable armrest. This should be the one room in the house where it doesn't matter if food is spilled, furniture is well worn, or the colors coordinate. The flowers in this room should be in abundance, outnumbered only by the candles that say, "Welcome home!"

There is one problem with decorating this room: there is a pooper at every party who tries to tear down the decorations! All of your marvelous intentions...just like that! Wham! Total and complete destruction! Satan sends circumstances our way to try and vandalize the family room of our heart.

He will whisper in your ear, “She doesn’t like you.” Pop! There goes one festively placed balloon!

“You don’t have as much money as they do!” All of that beautifully twisted crepe paper comes ripping off the ceiling.

“Her husband got a promotion and yours did not. Nothing ever goes right for you!” All of the lovely flowers in all of the well-placed vases start to wilt!

“Her children are so much better behaved than yours are!” Splat! There appears a dark stain on the brand-new carpet.

“God must love her more than He loves you. She has children, and you are infertile!” Another stain! Right in the center of the room!

Satan wants to turn your party into a pity party. Satan’s plan is that you would decorate this room based upon circumstantial evidence. God has a different plan, however, and His plan is that this room will be a glorious reflection of the relationship that you have with Him! This room filled with *zoe* life and shouting with the abundance of joy, laughter, and music is only beautiful because of Him, your Creator God!

> You will make known to me the path of life. In your presence is fullness of joy; at Your right hand there are pleasures forever.
> – **PSALM 16:11**

The truth is that you had absolutely nothing to do with the decorations in the family room of your heart. This room does not boast of your color scheme and is probably not your style at all. He chose it all because in His presence is fullness of joy! This room does not look like you at all - it was meant to look like Him!

***Buy Doughnuts!***

Ah-h-h-h-h! I hate this part! I despise it and loathe it with a passion! I am not a good cook...I hate to cook...I never know what to fix...I am a rotten cook...I have no culinary skills whatsoever... What? You think that I am whining? Well, suffice it to say, next time I invite you over for dinner, you might want to suggest that we order out!

Seriously, I never know what to fix when I invite people into my home. My kitchen shelf is filled with a rare assortment of very fine cookbooks. I have French cookbooks, Southern cookbooks, low-carb cookbooks, church cookbooks, country cookbooks, illustrated cookbooks, old-fashioned cookbooks, Weight Watcher's cookbooks! Sadly, I confess, very few of them have ever even been opened! Ah-h-h-h-h! What in the world am I doing entertaining?! I always spend way too much money on the food for a party in my home. I usually end up buying a new cookbook... (Yeah! Right! Like that will solve my problem!) Then I choose something much too exotic to fix...buy spices I have never heard of...and create a royal mess in my kitchen!

When Craig and I were preparing to move to Mobile, Alabama, and embark on a calling to pastor in the local church, I met with a seasoned pastor's wife. She and her husband had served the Lord faithfully in church after church all over the Midwest. She was a woman whom I respected spiritually and admired as a role model. I sat down with this great woman of God and innocently asked, "Do you have any advice for me on how to be a good pastor's wife?"

She looked straight into my soul and answered without a moment of hesitation, "Buy doughnuts!"

After I gulped a few times and tried not to look at her as if the ministry had finally caused her to lose her holy marbles, she patiently explained that the ministry was not about pretense. She encouraged me never to live my life in such a way that I was trying to impress the people in our local church. She encouraged me to be myself, to live life easily, and to feel free to buy doughnuts! I loved her for it, and I have never forgotten her valuable advice. Now it is my turn to give advice, and I have told that story to many young pastor's wives. It bodes well for all of us...not just for those who have a pastor for a husband. Never try to impress or be something that you are not. If cooking is your thing, then you go ahead and bake your little heart out, girl! But if you do something else well, take pleasure in your gifts and talents, and do not compare yourself with the Betty Crocker of the church world. See you on the doughnut aisle!

The Lord spoke to me through my friend, the seasoned pastor's wife, because I realized that I did not have to strain and struggle to impress. All I had to do was make a guest list, clean up my act, plan a date on the calendar, and decorate my life with His presence! He would be providing the food that would last a lifetime!

Psalm 34:8 says, "O taste and see that the LORD is good." You are in for a treat when you choose to feast on all that He is! What a delicacy! When He provides the meal for your party, it will make peanut butter and jelly seem like surf and turf! We should be feasting on the Lamb of God who takes away the sins of the world and the bread of His Word as well! Jesus said in John 6:35, "I am the bread of life; he who comes to Me will not hunger, and he who believes in me will never thirst." The life that Jesus is referring to in this passage is not *bios* or *psuche* life, but it is *zoe* life! He is the bread of *zoe* life! When Jesus is the guest of honor at your party, it absolutely does not matter what else happens, because He will provide for all of your needs!

Jesus, His mother, and His disciples were on the guest list to a wedding in Cana of Galilee. The host of this wedding ran out of wine long before it was time for the reception to be over. This caused the host, the bride, and the groom to be placed in an extremely embarrassing position. Mary, the mother of Jesus, may have known this family well because it was at her prompting that Jesus was asked to help out in this dilemma. Although Jesus resisted, presumably because He did not want attention drawn to Himself at this time, He instructed the servants to bring to Him six pots of water. After the servants had obeyed the request of Jesus, He told them to check the contents of these earthen containers. The servants were in for the shock of their lives! Instead of water inside the pots, there was now very fine wine! Instead of the ordinary substance merely drawn from the well, there was a beverage of great expense and pleasure. The water in the clay pots had turned into wine at the sound of Jesus' voice! (See John 2:1-10.)

Jesus will take all of the ordinary things of your life and turn them into something extraordinary! It is just His nature to take the boring and mundane and turn it into something miraculous! Jesus will turn all of your water into wine! As the sound of His voice, water always becomes the best wine of life! At the sound of His voice, your ordinary life becomes the extraordinary *zoe* life!

### *The Music of Life*

The final component to your *zoe* life party is the best part of all! We have to plan some activities to make the family room of your heart a happening place! What is a party without music? And games?

Don't you dare forget the gifts! And let's dance long into the night! Have you ever noticed how music really does set the atmosphere? Every member of my family is a music-holic; we are absolutely addicted to music! If country music is playing in the car, I'll be slapping my leg but definitely not singing along! Every Friday is Oldies Day in the McLeod Mobile. And so on Friday, I feel a bit younger and my heart turns to those bittersweet days of youth. The songs from the '60s and '70s have a special place in my memory, and hearing Karen Carpenter sing about "Rainy Days and Mondays" never fails to take my heart back to high school basketball games, slumber parties, and the hallways of my alma mater.

Maybe you will play classical music at your party, and I will undoubtedly wish that I had dressed up just a bit more. Perhaps I should have worn my white gloves, and I will certainly use my very best grammar! If jazz is the music of choice at your party, I will be wishing that I wasn't raised Pentecostal so that I knew how to dance! However, even I have my musical limits! If you even dare to play one rap song...I'm outta here! I'll kiss this party one quick good-bye!

What kind of music is playing at your party in the family room of your heart? I hope that it is music that brings glory to Jesus, otherwise your party will be over before it has even begun! It doesn't matter if the style is old hymns on a Hammond B-52 organ or if you are jammin' with Jesus on an electric guitar. It doesn't matter if you are joining Andy Griffith in crooning about "The Old Rugged Cross" or you are just delirious with Delirious...what matters is that you are making melody in your heart to the Lord.

> Speaking to one another in psalms and hymns and spiritual songs, singing and making melody with your heart to the Lord. – **EPHESIANS 5:19**

The Greek actually gives the word picture of the above verses that the heart is a stringed instrument and that we are to strum the strings of our hearts, which will result in celebration! You need to start strumming those strings of your heart...some of your heart-strings are out of tune...but you can do it! Just start right now! Start singing softly. Pretty soon the music will grow into a solid song of praise, and, before you know it, you will be lifting your voice in a mighty chorus of praise to the One who gives a song in the night!

> The LORD will command His lovingkindness in the daytime; and His song will be with me in the night, a prayer to the God of my life. – **PSALM 42:8**

***Be a Giver Not a Taker***

Every child in every country from every generation knows that the best part of the entire party is when the host says, "OK, it's now time for the gifts!" Pandemonium breaks out, resulting in rip-roaring hilarity! God loves a hilarious giver, and you will never tap into *zoe* life until you start giving with heartfelt generosity. God created you to be a giver, not a taker, and you absolutely cannot come to a party given in God's honor with empty hands! People with true *zoe* life find that they actually pattern their life around the joy in giving out of their need, not out of their abundance. You will never tap into *zoe* life if you do not start giving and serving today! Every morning when you wake up, remind yourself that you are a giver, not a taker, and that you are intent on looking for every possible opportunity to give to someone today. Bake a loaf of bread...make a phone call...take a friend to lunch...write a note of encouragement...offer to take care of someone's children...fix a meal for a busy wife. You will find inexpressible purpose and joy when you begin to give your life away!

***"May I Have This Dance?"***

I have a sad but true confession to make. I cannot dance. I never took dance lessons. I was never in a ballet recital. I can count to four, but my feet have not yet found the pattern. Rumba? Cha-Cha? Waltz? They are all foreign words to me! I was raised in a conservative, Pentecostal home, and the word "dance" just was not in our vocabulary. We played games, had friends over often, ate great food, decorated for every imaginable holiday...but we never danced! I will let you in on a small secret: often, late at night, when the children were supposed to be in bed, I would hear the strains of the Irving Berlin song "Always" winding its way up the stairs. I would quietly creep down the stairs and breath a sigh of childhood contentment as I watched my mother dancing in my father's arms. My father was a closet dancer! He danced as smoothly and as effortlessly as Fred Astaire!

My feet did not inherit my father's dance gene, but in my heart I dance all the time! I watch the young girls on the worship team and try to figure out how in the world they are dancing, staying on pitch, and holding a microphone! I finally realized that the secret is to bend your knees and then lift your hands in the air. How easy is that? If you do not know how to dance, here is my advice for you: start imitating the dance in someone else's life! Before long, you will have figured out their secret, and you will be dancing on your own!

Because of my choreographed-impaired childhood, I know that I will never be the girl who gets Gene Kelly or John Travolta. That's just fine with me, though, because I will be the girl who gets Jesus!

He will be my dance partner through all of life!

> And David was dancing before the LORD with all his might, and David was wearing a linen ephod. So David and all the house of Israel were bringing up the ark of the LORD with shouting and the sound of trumpet. – **2 SAMUEL 6:14-15**

David was wearing a linen ephod, which was the garment of a priest, as he danced before the Lord with all his might! This was an incredible fact to my little Pentecostal, conservative brain - priests dance before the Lord with all their might! We, as God's children, are a royal priesthood, and we need to dance with all our might! If you are who the Bible says you are, then you better start learning the cha-cha, because it is time to dance before the Lord with all your might!

> You have turned for me my mourning into dancing.
> – **PSALM 30:11**

Do you know why He turned your mourning into dancing? He is looking at you...deep within your heart...smiling gently and softly asking, "May I have this dance?" Jesus wants to be the One who will dance with you through all of life's music. He took all of the circumstances of your life that were causing indescribable pain and turned the sorrow into a song of love. He wants to be the Guest of Honor at your party, to decorate your heart with His love, and to give you something to sing about. Jesus wants you to feast on His presence.

Did Someone just tap you on the shoulder? Will you dance with Him?

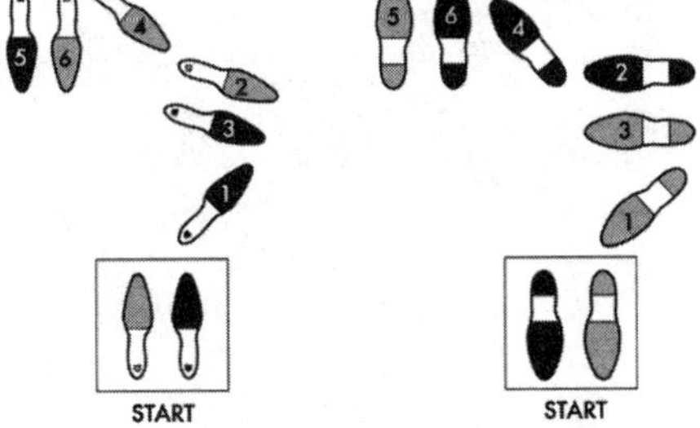

# Chapter Eight

# THE PRAYER CLOSET

> But you, when you pray, go into your inner room, close your door and pray to your Father who is in secret, and your Father who sees what is done in secret will reward you.
> **– MATTHEW 6:6**

Tucked away in the bowels of your heart is a place that only you and God go. It is a quiet place, full of peace. This peace rules and reigns supreme in your heart, yet still your heart is where battles are fought and victories won. In this solitary place, innermost secrets are revealed and desires are delicately whispered. It is here that righteousness is imputed and birthright demanded! This room has a solitary high-back chair that is accompanied only by a nightstand on which sits a lamp with a dimly lit bulb. A Bible and a well-worn prayer journal sit lovingly on the floor beside the nightstand. The rug in front of the chair has two worn spots where years of staying on your knees before God have imprinted the carpet. The walls are barren because no decorations are necessary. Creature comforts are totally ignored in this closet of prayer, and no signs of extravagance or personality have been added. This room is all about spirit – it is where my spirit touches the Spirit of God. This room is where I reach up to heaven, while standing on my tiptoes, and stretch with every ounce of human energy. He reaches down, scoops me into His lap, and touches my humanity with His divinity. The touching of my spirit with His Spirit becomes an embrace that will last for all of eternity. The prayer closet of my heart is where my heart touches the heart of God and lingers.

### *The Command Center*

The prayer closet is, in reality, a mere façade. What you see in the prayer closet is not actually what you get. It is not what you think it is, because, really, your prayer closet is not simple, nor is it solitary. Your prayer closet is not a place of undisturbed peace. Your prayer closet is the command center of operations for every single event that you experience in life. It is the nerve center, or the brain, for every person, every relationship, every situation, every circumstance, and every concern that enters your life. When you think that all you are doing is whispering a prayer, all of heaven stands at attention! Every angel starts barking orders and begins to rearrange meetings on your behalf. Divine appointments are made and history is literally changed because you uttered a prayer! You do not realize the power that you have in prayer, because if you did, you would spend your life on your face in your prayer closet. When you call on the name of Jesus and simply follow it with the two words "Help me," all of the angels and archangels, all of the heavenly warriors who battle on your behalf, rush to the throne and wait for further instructions!

***The Object of Your Devotion***

The one question that remains is, "Will you pray?"

The apostle Paul wrote in Colossians 4:2, "Devote yourselves to prayer, keeping alert in it with an attitude of thanksgiving." To what are you devoted? To the acquiring of money or to your job? I am devoted to my children and my marriage. Some women are devoted to clothes or their home, others to education or prestige. Regardless of where your devotion lies, I can guarantee that you will spend time doing that to which you are devoted!

Craig and I are up to our necks in the ministry, and we love every single second of it! We are training our children to love people and to love God. It is a family call and a heritage that we hope to pass down to the generations to come. But (you knew there was a but, didn't you?) when Duke University or the University of North Carolina is playing basketball, either we are on the family room floor screaming our brains out or our VCR is set so we can watch the game later that night. We are devoted to ACC basketball...what can I say? You will spend time doing that to which you are devoted!

The Bible commands us to be devoted to prayer! Why did God, through Paul, call us to this particular devotion? Did God want us to spend our lives cloistered in a closet away from the world? Absolutely not! God commands us to choose a devotion to prayer so that we can make a difference in the world!

### *The Power of Forgiveness*

Jesus gave us the model of how we should pray in Matthew 6:9-13. This is the most famous prayer that has ever been prayed. It is known quite simply, yet profoundly, as "The Lord's Prayer."

*Our Father who is in heaven, hallowed be Your name. Your kingdom come, Your will be done, on earth as it is in heaven. Give us this day our daily bread. And forgive us our debts, as we also have forgiven our debtors. And do not lead us into temptation, but deliver us from evil. For Yours is the kingdom and the power and the glory forever. Amen.*

This is the prayer that has stood the test of time for over two millennia. Songs have been written based upon this prayer, and lives have been built around the content of this prayer. It is the most familiar of all spoken prayers through all of written history. But just because it is familiar does not mean that we understand it. When this prayer is closely examined, there is a key to prayer that is enveloped in the middle of the verbiage. "Forgive us our debts, as we also have forgiven our debtors." Forgiveness is the human key to prayer!

> For if you forgive others for their transgressions, your heavenly Father will also forgive you. But if you do not forgive others, then your Father will not forgive your transgressions.
> – **MATTHEW 6:14-15**

The only point that Jesus reiterated outside of the context of the exact prayer is the importance of forgiveness. When Jesus tells you to do something two times in one breath, my advice to you is this: Just do it!

I believe that prayers go unanswered and are certainly not as powerful as they have the potential to be if prayed with unforgiveness in our hearts. Prayer will not yield the results you desire if you are holding bitterness or anger in your heart toward a sister or a brother in the Lord. These verses clearly say that there is a correlation between our forgiveness of others and the Father's ability to forgive us. These verses are not referring to salvation...but to forgiveness. These are verses of discipline in a Christian's life and are a tenet of Christianity that must be embraced.

If you sow forgiveness to others, then you will reap forgiveness from your Father. The profound Kingdom principle is this: You will always reap what you have sown. If you sow mercy, you will reap mercy (Matt. 5:7). If you sow judgment, you will reap judgment (Matt. 7:1). So often we think of this principle only in terms of sowing our tithe and then reaping a harvest with a raise at work...or a bonus...or winning the lottery. This principle rings true in every single attitude sown, every hour spent in prayer, and in every fruit of the Spirit that we share with others. You absolutely will reap what you sow!

> Whenever you stand praying, forgive, if you have anything against anyone, so that your Father who is in heaven will also

forgive you your transgressions. But if you do not forgive, neither will your Father who is in heaven forgive your transgressions. – **MARK 11:25-26**

Forgiveness is the serious business of Christianity and is not to be glossed over lightly. Grace is not cheap, and you must always bear in mind that Jesus paid an enormously high price for you, which requires you to forgive all the time! Forgiveness is one of the most important tenets of Christianity that demands that we, as His children, do not hold grudges. We are not a bitter people, and we certainly do not look for the opportunity for revenge. Christians always forgive and look for opportunities to bless those who have wronged them. We obey God, and we pray for our enemies! It is just how we do life!

It does not matter what someone did or what he or she said, nor does it matter how they acted or what they thought. What matters is that you forgive! I can guarantee that you are holding back a blessing in life if you choose not to forgive. Can you forgive the boss who needlessly fired your husband? Or the drunk driver who killed someone whom you loved very much? Can you forgive the other woman? Can you forgive a crabby mother-in-law or a husband who has been abusive for thirty years? What about the coach who did not play your child or the man who broke your heart?

Craig and I have learned that in marriage, the first one to forgive wins! I love winning, so I will always forgive! I have learned that it is more fun to forgive than it is to be crippled by grudges and bitterness! If you can forgive freely and lovingly, it will free you to serve God and reach new levels of power in the prayer closet.

Forgiveness is so important to God that He sent His only Son to die on your behalf. Forgiving you cost God dearly. Forgiveness always entails a death...and a price. Are you willing to die to your own hurts and your own wounds and just simply forgive? It will cost you to forgive. The price that you will pay to forgive is called humility. You will need to humble yourself and choose to forgive if you want your prayers to bear the effective results that you so desire. Jesus humbled Himself so that you could be forgiven, and you must do things God's way in order to cash in on the blessings of God!

You might be thinking, Carol, you don't understand! I am not perfect! If you are talking about perfection, then my prayers will never be answered, because perfection is a long-distance phone call for me!

Perfection is not the goal...forgiveness is. When I approach the throne of God in prayer carrying unforgiveness in my heart toward a person who was made in the image of God, then there will be a blockage. My prayers will be hindered by a detour or perhaps a huge roadblock. When I come to God with guile in my heart toward a person in my life, God says to me, "Go and forgive them, and then we will talk."

If you are a parent, you will understand this principle that is birthed in the heart of our Father God. If one of my five children is angry with one of their siblings and refuses to mend the relationship, it will certainly affect the manner in which I deal with the angry child. What if the angry child comes to me and says, "Mama! I love you so much! I am so glad that you are my mama! Even though I hate my brother, can I still have a brand-new bike?"

My response will be quick and sure. "No, son. Let's settle the issue with your brother, and then we will talk about the bike."

Jesus cares about our relationships more than He cares about our requests. James 5:9 explains it this way, "Do not complain, brethren, against one another, so that you yourselves may not be judged; behold, the Judge is standing right at the door."

If you have felt the freedom of God's forgiveness...the unbridled joy that comes with a heart that is clean...the exhilaration of emancipation...certainly you will be thrilled to forgive others! You are acting just like Jesus when you forgive others!

> Then Peter came up to Him and said, "Lord, how often shall my brother sin against me and I forgive him? Up to seven times?" Jesus said to him, "I do not say to you, up to seven times, but up to seventy times seven." – **MATTHEW 18:21-22**

Peter thought he was hot stuff! He thought that he was going to impress the Messiah with his understanding of the very spiritual trait of forgiveness. The number seven was a religious number, and Peter was strutting his stuff when he brought up the number seven in the presence of Perfection Himself! Seven was the perfect number, and Peter thought that he had the perfect answer! When Jesus responded that he should forgive with the impossible number of up to seventy times seven, it let all the hot air out of Peter's bloated balloon! Jesus was saying, in effect, "Peter, it is My perfect plan for you to forgive to infinity and beyond!"

> The sacrifice of the wicked is an abomination to the LORD, but the prayer of the upright is His delight. – **PROVERBS 15:8**

God is absolutely delighted when you come to Him with peace in all of your relationships! He is thrilled to hear from you and to answer you when you love Him enough to love the people that He has placed in your world!

This Bible truth is evident and straightforward time after time after time. There is a blessing that inevitably follows when you are able to forgive someone who has wronged you. The blessing is this: God will pay attention to you! He will forgive you your sins, there will be absolutely no blockage in your relationship with Him, and He will hear your prayers!

> The LORD is far from the wicked, but He hears the prayers of the righteous. – **PROVERBS 15:29**

As you spend some time in the prayer closet of your heart, settle the issue right now. Whom do you need to forgive? Who has wronged you that you need to forgive? Who has disappointed you that you need to forgive? Who has hurt or mistreated or ignored you that you just simply need to forgive? If you can show mercy and forgive the people in your life who have wronged you, God will be delighted with your prayers! Your time in the prayer closet will be productive and powerful!

> We know that God does not hear sinners; but if anyone is God fearing and does His will, He hears him. – **JOHN 9:31**

***The Power of Believing***

When you pray, believe that God hears you! It is time for you to be done with wimpy, half-hearted prayers uttered from a heart full of doubt and maybe's. It is time for you to be bold in the prayer closet of your heart and believe that He is well able to answer you! Jesus at one point during His earthly life was summoned to the bedside of His dear friend, Lazarus. Lazarus was very ill, and his sisters, Martha and Mary, sent for the One whom they loved as well. Mary and Martha knew that Jesus was the answer to their prayers, and they sent an urgent message that He should come immediately. Jesus loved Mary and Martha, but when He heard that Lazarus was sick, He willfully decided to stay two days longer in the place where He was! What kind of friend would do that? What kind of love would stay away by a decisive choice when a loved one was facing death?

You may have asked that question many times in the prayer closet of your heart: "Jesus, if You love me, why aren't You running to take care of me? Why aren't You answering my request?"

Because Jesus did not go immediately to the home of Lazarus in the dusty little town of Bethany, Lazarus died. The situation went from bad to worse. Have you ever felt that way? That Jesus, in spite of your prayers, has allowed your circumstances to grow exponentially more horrible by the day? What kind of loving God does this? He could snap His fingers and change the circumstances! Why won't He?

Maybe the reason that He does not answer on our time schedule is because He is on a different schedule altogether with an entirely different plan. In the case of Lazarus, Jesus wanted to show His glory, not His punctuality.

Jesus arrived in Bethany to a scene of sheer pandemonium. The mourners were out in full force, Martha was outraged with grief, and Lazarus was in the grave. As Jesus arrived at the cave where Lazarus had been buried, He spoke to the people gathered around and commanded them to remove the stone. Jesus said this with great confidence and authority as if this were an everyday happening.

Martha, the busy sister...the practical one...the worry-wart...the realist, spoke to Jesus and said, "You are too late, Lord! This situation is even out of Your control! If You have the stone removed, the stink is going to blow us all out of Bethany!" I am sure that you have never even thought of speaking to Jesus in such a manner! When you have been disappointed with the plan of God, how have you responded? Have you responded with great trust and faith...or with accusations and words of frustration?

Remember also that when you call out to God and ask for His divine intervention in the chaos of your life, there will be well-meaning people who will remind you of the facts. Faith is a foreign word to realists, but we chose to walk by faith not by facts. We take great joy in walking by faith...not by sight...and certainly not by smell!

After Craig and I had been married for three years, we became pregnant with our first child. Although the pregnancy was precarious, on January 29, 1981, I gave birth to our first son, Matthew Craig McLeod. Two years later, while living in Buffalo, we were blessed with Christopher Burton McLeod on the snowy morning of January 27, 1983. When Christopher was two years old, we decided that it was time to enlarge our family, and we quickly found out that I was pregnant. This pregnancy ended in miscarriage and nearly broke my heart. But we were determined that it was God's will for us to have more children, and so I was soon pregnant again. Miscarriage followed miscarriage, and I was tottering on the precipice of depression. It was during the struggle with infertility that Craig and I and our two sons relocated to North Carolina. Craig was called to pastor a church in the Raleigh area, and we were thrilled to be in close proximity to Durham where Duke University has gained an international reputation for its medical center. We were able to be treated at the Duke Infertility Clinic and had great hope that these world-famous doctors would soon have an answer for us.

In the summer of 1987, after suffering my fourth miscarriage, one of the women from our church approached me on a Sunday morning. She was dressed in self-righteous pretense while I was dressed in pain. She had all the answers and I had only questions. This church woman, who had her name etched in gold on the front pew, announced to me, "Well, Carol, now you know that it is not God's will."

I looked at her through my incredulous tears and innocently asked, "What is not God's will?"

"Now you know that it is not God's will for you to have any more children," she pronounced with prophetic glee.

It was all that I could do to hold back the tears...the rage...and some very improper words for a pastor's wife! I knew no such thing, and I was not about to buy into her negative worldview! Her words, however, propelled me into fighting mode, and I put on my spiritual boxing gloves and began fighting for all that I was worth! My spiritual dukes were up because Satan was not about to steal future babies from me; I was ready to wage war in the heavenlies.

My prayer life grew in faith and in boldness. I fell in love with Jesus in my prayer closet as He lovingly shaped me into the woman who could serve Him wholeheartedly. Depression was not an option any longer because of the joy I discovered while basking in His presence!

On September 2, 1988, Jordan Reid McLeod brought his special brand of enthusiasm and creativity to our home, and we have never been the same since! Carolyn Joy McLeod arrived on February 4, 1991, and her little girl ways have sweetened our home with music and laughter. Joni Rebecca McLeod was our darling surprise, and all of our hearts have been wrapped around her little fingers ever since that spring day in 1994 when she first opened her big blue eyes. What was God's will for me in the midst of miscarriage...in the ocean of depression and doubt? God's will for me was to fight with faith! God's will for me was to fall in love with Him! God's will for my life was to realize that my life was about His presence, not about His presents!

> Jesus said to her, "Did I not say to you that if you believe, you will see the glory of God?" – **JOHN 11:40**

You have to believe if you desire to experience His glory in your circumstances. Believing is a prerequisite to the glory of God being revealed in your chaos!

> So they removed the stone. Then Jesus raised His eyes and said, "Father, I thank You that You have heard Me. I knew that You always hear Me; but because of the people standing around I said it, so that they may believe that You sent Me."
> – **JOHN 11:41-42**

What an audacious faith Jesus had! He verbalized His full confidence that God heard every word that was spoken from the mouth and heart of Jesus. Jesus came to His Father with boldness and faith! You can and should come to your Father with the exact same boldness. God hears every word that you speak in the prayer closet of your heart. Thank Him for hearing you! When you call out to God, it is imperative that you believe that He hears every word whispered in His presence.

In Hebrews 4, Jesus invites us to come to His throne fearlessly, confidently, and boldly. It is His heartfelt desire that you would not come with doubts or with fears, but that you would come with full assurance and believe that He is who He says He is and that He can do what He says that He can do! Verse 16 says that the result of coming to the throne of grace with great boldness is that we will find help at exactly the right time and for every need that we have. It is God's express will for us to enter His presence not as whining wimps but as warriors!

Not only does Jesus invite you to come to His throne room confidently and boldly, but He has also given you a spirit of power so that you would come in the manner that He has requested! Second Timothy 1:7 reminds us that God does not give us a spirit of timidity or of cowardice. God gives to His children a powerful spirit, and it is with that power we are to approach His throne. Jesus would never ask you to do something for which He has not already made provision!

> Now faith is the assurance of things hoped for, the conviction of things not seen....And without faith it is impossible to please Him, for he who comes to God must believe that He is and that He is a rewarder of those who seek Him.
>
> – **HEBREWS 11:1, 6**

If your desire is to please God in the prayer closet of your heart, then you must come in faith. If you come to God in faith, you will be well pleasing to Him, and He will reward your faith! I preface nearly every prayer that I pray with these simple sentences, "I believe You, God! I have faith!" I want my Father to know from the very beginning of my prayer that the reason I am boldly coming to Him is because my prayer life is about Him...not about me!

Did you know that it says in Mark 11 that our faith has the capability of moving mountains? What an extravagant possibility! However, just as with all of the promises of God, this one comes with a string attached. The only way that we will move mountains with our faith is if we do not doubt!

If you want to accomplish great things with your faith, you must settle the issue of your doubts. You cannot believe in God half the time...or believe that your life is some game of cosmic roulette. You must believe without doubting and without wavering! This is the God of all creation in Whom you are placing your trust! This is the God who sent His only Son to die on the cross so that you could live forever! This is the same God who parted the Red Sea, made water come from the rock, gave little David the power to slay a mighty giant, and who raised Lazarus from the dead! Do not allow your doubts to rule your faith! Allow your faith to rule your doubts!

After Jesus, in Mark 11, encourages believers to pray in faith, then He says that we also must forgive if we desire power in our prayer life. Jesus says that, in order to get results from our prayers, forgiveness is every bit as powerful as faith. These verses actually say that we are to forgive anything we have against anyone! (See Mark 11:22-26.)

These verses in Scripture give stability to the call to pray with bold faith. Faith is not the entirety of prayer; faith is always coupled with forgiveness. Faith and forgiveness are tandem traits of prayer.

You will have no power to speak to a mountain if your heart is full of unforgiveness.

> This is the confidence that we have in Him, that if we ask anything according to His will, He hears us. And if we know that He hears us, whatever we ask, we know that we have the petitions that we have asked of Him. – **1 JOHN 5:14-15, NKJV**

I love those scriptures! First John 5:14-15 just may be my very favorite praying scriptures in the whole Bible! If I pray according to God's will, I know that I know that I know that He hears me! If He hears me, I know that He is going to answer my request in the affirmative! This is the secret to having the knowledge that He hears me and that He is certain to answer: I must pray according to the will of God! How easy is that? Praying according to God's will is pure joy and always yields great results! Allow me to illustrate...

The Bible says that it is not His will that any should perish (2 Pet. 3:9). Because I know that this is His will, when I pray for someone to be saved, I know that He hears me and that His answer is on the way. His response to a prayer that someone should be saved is this, "You got it! Coming right up!" Do you understand the power in that? I prayed according to the will of God...I believed that He heard my voice...His answer is music to my earthly ears!

The psalmist wrote in Psalm 103:3, "Bless the LORD, O my soul! And all that is within me, bless His holy name. Bless the

LORD, O my soul, and forget none of His benefits; who pardons all your iniquities, who heals all your diseases." It is imperative to believe that God's will is found in His Word. When you believe that, praying for healing becomes pure delight! I believe that every single word in the Word is true! I believe it with every breath that I take and every day that I live. So - when I pray for someone to be healed from a sickness, I am praying according to God's will because this verse in Psalms clearly states that He heals ALL your diseases.

I have faith when I pray for the sick to be healed because I want to please God with my faith. When I lay hands on someone and pray for a physical healing, I pray with these words, "Lord, I know that You are well able to heal this disease. I know that You can heal! So I ask You, Lord, would You heal? I know that You can heal...I ask You, Lord...will You heal?"

When I come to God and ask for pink Cadillacs, vacation homes, new jobs, and husbands...I cannot come with the same boldness that I possess when I know that something is the will of God according to the Word of God. Who knows about cars, the Caribbean, careers, and hunks? I just know about the Word! Seek His will in His Word, and you will begin to know Him intimately. When you touch the heart of God, you will have the holy audacity to enter in with boldness! If you know His Word, then you will know His will. If you are struggling with the eternal question, "Is this God's will for my life?", then let me encourage you to become a student of the Bible.

Psalm 119:105 says, "Your word is a lamp to my feet and a light to my path." His Word will even give you direction concerning how you should pray. If you are struggling with your time in the prayer closet of your heart, then just settle down in the rocking chair, turn on the lamp, and open the Word. Prayer will become a delight when oiled with the direction of the Word of God!

### *Be a Pest to God!*

Would you please make yourself a pest to God? Will you be an advocate of persistent, consistent prayer? Never, never, never give up in the prayer closet of your heart.

> Now He was telling them a parable to show that at all times they ought to pray and not to lose heart, saying, "In a certain city there was a judge who did not fear God and did not respect man. There was a widow in that city, and she kept coming to him, saying, 'Give me legal protection from my opponent.' For a while he was unwilling; but afterward he said to himself, 'Even though I do not fear God nor respect man, yet because this widow bothers me, I will give her legal protection, otherwise by continually coming she will wear me out.'" – **LUKE 18:1-5**

It was important for Jesus to encourage us in the issues of prayer, and this parable is meant to encourage us in persistent prayer. This is the story of a corrupt judge who cared nothing for God or man. (Sounds like some of our politicians today, doesn't it?) A widow who needed a restraining order against a legal enemy wouldn't let this judge alone until he gave her what she needed! This wearisome widow got in the judge's face until he got so tired of her that he gave her what she wanted! How encouraging to know that the Man who hears our requests loves us dearly and desires to bless us! Get on your knees and get in God's face until He answers you!

> Ask, and it will be given to you; seek, and you will find; knock, and it will be opened to you. For everyone who asks receives,

and he who seeks finds, and to him who knocks it will be opened. – **MATTHEW 7:7-8**

The verb tense used in the writing of these verses indicates the importance of persistent and consistent prayer. A better translation of these verses would be, "Ask, and keep on asking! Seek, and keep on seeking! Knock, and keep on knocking!" God will answer the believer who consistently and persistently asks...seeks...and knocks! Asking...and then seeking...and then knocking...is called prayer! I have purposed in my heart that I will never give up in the prayer closet of my heart. I might cry, but I won't whine...I might be a pest, but I won't be impatient...I might grow weary, but I will never give up!

When you are diligent and when you persevere, you prove something to God! You prove that you are serious and that you are well aware of the fact that He is your only hope. You have nowhere else to turn...nowhere else to go. A doctor does not have the answer that you want...a banker only gives words of disappointment and pain...computer dating services are not for you...and Weight Watchers has let you down again! When you are determined to spend your life in the prayer closet of your heart, if that is what it takes, you are yelling to every angel in heaven and every demon in hell, "This is not some cosmic game of hide and seek! I am boldly coming to my Father! I am coming in faith, and this mountain is about to move!"

The effective prayer of a righteous man can accomplish much. – **JAMES 5:16**

The word fervent in this verse can also be translated as "diligent." The problem with most of us, as twenty-first century

Christians in the Western world, is that we could not define the word diligent if our last name was Webster! We enjoy instant mashed potatoes...we cook three-hour meals in twenty minutes in the microwave oven...and at least three times a week, we drive up to the fast-food window and order fast food! Fast-food restaurants so fan the flame of the spirit of expediency in us that we don't even get out of the car and complain when our meal takes longer than three minutes to be shoved out of the window! We live in modular homes that were thrown up in a week or less, and even use instant curl gel on our hair! Prepare yourself to be blown out of your microwave existence: God is not instant! In fact, God loves taking His time because He has all of eternity! With God, you absolutely cannot punch in the buttons and then stand in front of the door of the prayer closet while tapping your impatient foot and watching the clock move around its eternal circuitous path!

So many of us are tempted when God does not answer on our time table to say, "OK, God! I forgave! I came boldly! Now it is Your turn! Do it right now!"

Prayer does not work like that because you are not in charge...God is in charge. Can you trust God? Can you trust Him that He will accomplish His will in His time? Many of us approach prayer like a two-year-old having a temper tantrum in Toys-R-Us. We think that if we yell loudly enough, do all of the correct choreography, and point to the approved toy that somehow, someway, He will give in. Prayer in its entirety is about God revealing His glory in our lives in His time.

E. Stanley Jones, the famous missionary of the twentieth century and a great man of prayer, said this, "If I throw out a boat hook from the boat and catch hold of the shore and pull, do I pull the shore to me, or do I pull myself to the shore? Prayer is not pulling God to my will, but the aligning of my will to the will of God."

***The Lessons of Prayer***

The prayer closet of your heart is the nerve center of all of the operations of your life. Your prayer closet is where the deep work of your life is completed. You become like Jesus in this room because of the call to forgiveness. You please Him and not yourself when you enter this room with faith! The prayer closet is where you allow Him to align your will to His. Of course, this might take some time depending upon how stubborn you are!

I have already shared with you the story of my multiple miscarriages. The pain was indescribable...the disappointment was overwhelming...and at times I thought that I was going to drown in the emotional abyss that the deaths of these babies was causing. I will always remember the night after my third miscarriage when Craig and I were driving home from the hospital. I had been nearly fifteen weeks pregnant when this baby died and quietly went back to heaven. It had been a long day of induced labor followed by a surgical procedure. My body was bleeding, my soul was bleeding, and I was just trying to breathe. I looked over at Craig in the stillness of the night and said to him, "God has my attention now. I just want to learn what He is trying to teach me."

What is God trying to teach you in the prayer closet of your heart? He is trying to teach you the value of forgiveness and to believe boldly and to come in faith. He is trying to teach you to be patient and to never, ever give up. If you can learn these well-taught lessons, you will be a powerful prayer warrior who changes history in the prayer closet of your heart! If you can absorb the truths that He is explaining to you, there will be no confusion in your nerve center of operations. Prayer is a powerful discipline of the Christian walk! You have power in the kingdom of God, and you access this power through prayer.

It's time to leave the prayer closet. As you slowly get up from kneeling in front of the chair and turn toward the door, you will see a mirror has been placed on the back of the door while you were praying. It is impossible to leave the room without taking a departing glance into the glass. As you look in the mirror, your breath catches and you look again. This time, your gaze lingers at the beloved face that is looking back at you. It is not your eyes that look back...but your eyes have become His eyes. It is not your smile...but His smile. It is no longer your face...but your features have become His features. In the prayer closet of your heart you have been changed. You have been changed in His image, and now...you look just like Him.

*Epilogue*

# HOME – WHERE YOUR STORY BEGINS

It's been quite a journey, hasn't it? This tour of your heart has taken you places you never expected to see. It has called you to clean up some corners of your heart that had become cluttered with the issues of life. This view of your heart has encouraged you to look deeper, try harder, and live more lavishly than ever before. It has caused some moments of reevaluation, remodeling, and eventual restoration. There have been times of pain involved in this virtual tour as well as vignettes of outrageous celebration and hope. Now, it is time to open the door of your heart from the inside out and let your life burst forth into all that God has for you in this season of your life.

Life is different for all of us. Some of you are blessed with a six-figure income, an academic pedigree that impresses any career opportunity that comes your way, and a lifestyle of ease and extravagance. But your heart longs for home.

Maybe you are called to marriage and motherhood and have traded in your makeup bag for a diaper bag. Instead of great vacations in exotic places, you are immersed in nursery rhymes, Cheerios, and dirty diapers. Your heart longs for home as well.

Perhaps the season of marriage, motherhood, and career is all behind you now. You only dream of significance and what "might have been." You wish that your life had turned out differently, and now it seems as if it is too late. It is home that your heart longs for also.

Do you long for children that never came? Or a husband to whom you could give your heart? Maybe you wish for health – or financial stability - or just a good friend. Life is different for all of

us, and the pain can be overwhelming in the comparison. What you really long for is not someone else's life...but for a heart that you can call home.

Home is the place of memories and stability. It should hold the security of unconditional love, peaceful moments in the midst of life's storms, and a joy that supersedes all disappointment. Your heart becomes all of that and more when you allow Christ to make your heart His home. He should be the sole owner of the heart that is determining all that your life is becoming. He deserves more than an hour every Sunday...or a quick prayer uttered in the midst of the busyness of your life. A home is what He longs for as well. It is His deepest desire to make your heart His home...His residence...His place of address.

Many of us "give our hearts to Jesus" or ask "Jesus into our hearts," and it becomes a one-time experience that does not change anything about the way that we live. Giving your heart to Jesus is the adventure of a lifetime! When you asked Jesus into your heart, you signed a lifetime contract that could not be made null and void! He made payment in full and took the lockbox off the door of your heart. Now, your heart is His home - it no longer belongs only to you! The solitude of home...the stability of home...the security of home...only become a reality when you allow Him to fill every room of your heart!

***More about Carol...***

Carol is married to Craig, her college sweetheart and love of her life. They are the parents of five children. Craig serves as pastor of The Tabernacle, a church with over 2000 members in Orchard Park, NY.

Their oldest son, Matthew is a summa cum laude graduate of Oral Roberts University, has been a sports writer for the Tulsa World and currently works at the University in Media Relations. Matthew's lovely wife, Emily, also graduated summa cum laude from ORU and is a much-welcomed addition to the family. Christopher, the second son, is a senior at ORU majoring in music. Christopher hopes to be a Christian rock star and start his own recording studio! The three younger children, Jordan, Joy-Belle and Joni Becca are home schooled and share in the joy of being a part of the raucous, loving McLeod clan!

Carol is an author and popular speaker at women's conferences and retreats, where she teaches the Word of God with great joy and enthusiasm. She also hosts highly successful Just Joy! Outreaches. Carol encourages and empowers women with passionate and practical biblical messages mixed with her own special brand of hope and humor, which are sure to find a home in every room of a woman's heart.

A graduate of Oral Roberts University with a degree in Music and English, Carol has the distinction of being both the first Women's Chaplain and the first woman to speak at the university's Vespers.